THE AUSTRALIAN
Women's Weekly
preserves
& conserves

acp
books

contents

Getting started 4

Jams, marmalades
and jellies 10

Chutneys, pickles
and relishes 48

Sauces 96

Drinks 108

Glossary 114

Conversion chart 117

Index 118

The oven temperatures in this book are for conventional ovens; if you have a fan-forced oven, decrease the temperature by 10-20 degrees.

getting started

Traditionally, preserving was done year-round, each season, to keep food until nature made it available next time. The methods of preserving in days gone by were often as simple as drying – either in the sun or in a warm area set aside for the purpose, or in a part of the kitchen where food was hung to dry. Smoking was, and still is, a popular method of preserving food, particularly different types of meat and seafood. Salting and curing in brine worked well for meat, too. This book is about preserving fruit and vegetables using more modern ingredients including sugar, oil and vinegar. Most of the recipes for jams, jellies, pickles and chutneys will last season to season, that is, for a year. The keeping qualities depend on just a few things – the vegetables or fruit should be perfect, the jars (and lids) in which the food is preserved must be sterilised properly, and not chipped or cracked, and the storage must be done properly. We have given conservatively short keeping times for the preserve recipes in this book, as it's impossible to make preserves in a completely sterile environment in a normal home. It's worth knowing that even if the preserve keeps for a year or even more, as it ages it will gradually change in colour and texture – usually becoming darker and thicker. The preserve is still fine to eat, providing it smells good and is mould-free.

There are a number of little, though important, things to know, to achieve success every time.

JAMS & CONSERVES

Jams and conserves can be made from just one or several types of fruit – sometimes a vegetable is included. A conserve is a jam that contains large pieces of fruit. The method used for all jams and conserves doesn't vary much at all. The fruit is cooked with or without liquid – usually water – depending on the type of fruit, until it is tender, then sugar is added and the mixture is cooked until it is thick but spreadable when it's at room temperature. A lot of jams simply become a thick, sweet fruit spread after cooking, others have larger pieces of fruit suspended in a clear syrup that jells at a temperature of around 105°C/220°F.

MARMALADES

Marmalades are jams based on citrus fruit, one type or several, and can have another non-citrus fruit or vegetable added. Generally, a little like a conserve, citrus rind is suspended in a clear syrup that jells at the same temperature as jams and conserves (105°C/220°F); marmalade should be spreadable at room temperature.

The word marmalade is said to derive from the Portuguese word for quince – marmelo.

Marmalade is the most popular and easiest type of jam to make as citrus fruit contains a good balance of acid and pectin – both necessary to make marmalade jell. Just about any citrus fruit or combination of citrus fruits will make good marmalade.

Here is a basic trusty 7-step method for making marmalade that works every time, so mix and match citrus fruit for some different flavour sensations.

1 **CHOOSE PERFECT**, slightly under-ripe fruit; wash and dry the fruit.
2 **HALVE AND QUARTER** the fruit; reserve any juice, any trimmings and all the seeds. Cut through the quarters to make the rind as thick or as thin as you like.
3 **COMBINE ANY TRIMMINGS** with the seeds in a muslin bag. Put the fruit, juice and muslin bag in a large non-metallic bowl. Add enough cold water to the bowl to barely cover the fruit and to make it just barely float. Cover the bowl, and stand it overnight.
4 **PUT THE UNDRAINED** fruit mixture into a small boiler, cover and bring the mixture to the boil over high heat; reduce the heat and simmer between 30 minutes to 1 hour, depending on the fruit, until the rind is tender and mushy.
5 **MEASURE THE FRUIT MIXTURE** using a heatproof jug, allow 1 cup of white granulated sugar to each cup of fruit mixture; return the fruit mixture and the sugar to the boiler – this mixture should not be more than 5cm (2 inches) deep.
6 **STIR THE MIXTURE** over a high heat, without boiling, until the sugar is dissolved. Boil the mixture rapidly until the marmalade will jell when tested on a cold saucer.
7 **REMOVE ANY SCUM** Stand the marmalade 10 minutes; remove and discard any scum from the surface of the marmalade, using a large metal spoon. Next, use a medium heatproof jug to pour the

hot jam into hot sterilised jars, seal while hot. Label and date the jars when cold and store them in a cool, dark place.

SUGAR

Sugar is the ingredient that preserves jams, jellies, conserves, marmalades, liqueurs and some sauces and syrups. When sugar is combined with an acid ingredient, such as vinegar or lemon juice, it preserves chutneys, pickles, sauces and some relishes.

Unless otherwise specified, use regular granulated white table sugar in the recipes in this book. Jams, conserves, marmalades and jellies will benefit by using this coarser sugar; they will be clearer and more sparkling. Make sure the sugar is dissolved at the stage the recipe indicates. Brush the grains that stick to the side of the pan and wooden spoon back into the mixture using a pastry brush dipped in cold water. Or, put the lid on the boiler to cover the hot mixture for a minute or so – this will cause condensation to be trapped under the lid and the drops of moisture formed will wash the sugar grains from the side of the pan back into the preserve mixture.

Warming sugar before it is added to the boiler will dissolve the sugar faster, and should result in a clearer jam or jelly. To do this, spread the sugar in a large baking dish, to a maximum depth of 2.5cm (1 inch). Warm it in an oven preheated to 150°C/300°F. Stir the sugar a few times to warm it through evenly. Brown sugar, which comes in various shades and flavours from

EQUIPMENT

There's no special equipment needed for making preserves, but probably the most important thing is the right pan. Choose a pan made from heavy aluminium, enamel or stainless steel; don't use copper or unsealed cast-iron pans, as the natural acids in fruit and vegetables will damage the surfaces of these pans, spoiling the flavour of the preserve. Don't leave preserve mixtures standing in aluminium pans for more than an hour; once again, natural acids could affect the surface of the pan and the flavour of the preserve.

In most recipes, about half of the liquid is evaporated during the final cooking process. To do this successfully, a large, wide-topped pan is essential. A large saucepan or small boiler is usually fine for most recipes. As a guide to the size of saucepan to use, the preserve mixture should not be more than 5cm (2 inches) deep after all the ingredients have been added to the pan. Most preserve recipes have a stage where they are cooked covered; the lid should be tight-fitting, as this is the stage where evaporation is not wanted. Any stirring of a preserve mixture should be done with a strong large, clean (fat- and flavour-free) wooden spoon.

It's important to use a sharp knife when chopping vegetables and fruit for preserves, particularly for any fine cutting of citrus fruit peel.

A candy thermometer takes the guess work out of jam making, but it's not essential. A digital thermometer is easy to use and read.

DO

CHOOSE THE BEST QUALITY, freshest fruit – slightly under-ripe is best – or vegetables; fresh-picked or harvested is the best. Damaged, bruised or fruit gathered from under the tree could result in mouldy preserves.

STAND MARMALADES, and some jams and conserves, after cooking to allow the pieces of fruit to settle and disperse through the syrup before bottling. This is important if the fruit pieces are large; the fruit will rise to the top of the jar if the jam is bottled too soon.

BE FUSSY ABOUT STERILISING JARS and lids. The jars should be hot when the hot preserve is poured into them; stand jars on a wooden board or a towel to insulate the jars and the surface under them.

FILL THE JARS TO THE TOP with the preserve; it will shrink slightly on cooling, leaving a small space between the lid and the top surface of the preserve. Seal the jars while hot.

MAKE ONLY SMALL AMOUNTS of jam at a time. The colour, flavour, quality and clarity will be better.

DON'T

INCREASE THE QUANTITIES of the recipes unless you have the right large equipment. During cooking, about half the liquid evaporates; a wide-topped boiler is ideal for making most preserves.

REDUCE THE SUGAR CONTENT Sugar is a preservative; preserves made without enough sugar will not keep.

USE JARS THAT ARE CRACKED or chipped. Cracked jars will break when hot preserves are poured into them, and chips could harbour bacteria.

light brown through to black, is mostly used in pickles, chutneys, sauces and relishes. The darker the sugar the richer the flavour. Darker sugars are less refined and tend to have molasses-like flavours.

VINEGAR

Use good-quality vinegar that contains at least 4% acetic acid; poor-quality vinegars contain less acetic acid and so are not good for preserving.

JARS

The jars must be glass and have no chips or cracks; the lids need to be tight-fitting. Usually the lids are made from metal – some poor quality metal lids might corrode if they touch the surface of the preserve during storage. If in doubt, place a disc of baking paper (parchment) inside the lid of the jar before securing. Metal lids that have a lining to prevent contact with the preserve are the best of all to use. Screw-top lids form a good seal on jars, clip-on plastic lids don't seal as well. Jars that have a clamped-down lid with a rubber seal also work well – it's important that the seal be tight-fitting and firm as old seals lose their grip and can perish in time. If in doubt, buy new rubber seals for the lids.

STERILISING JARS

It's important the jars be as clean as possible; make sure your hands, the preparation area, tea towels and cloths etc, are clean, too. The aim is to finish sterilising the jars and lids at the same time the preserve is ready to be bottled; the hot preserve should be bottled into hot, dry clean jars. Jars that aren't sterilised properly can cause deterioration of the preserves during storage.

Here are three methods for sterilising jars. Always start with cleaned washed jars and lids.

1 **PUT THE JARS AND LIDS** through the hottest cycle of a dishwasher without using any detergent.

2 **LIE THE JARS DOWN** in a boiler with the lids, cover them with cold water then cover the boiler with a lid. Bring the water to the boil over a high heat and boil the jars for 20 minutes.

3 **STAND THE JARS UPRIGHT,** without touching each other, on a wooden board on the lowest shelf in the oven. Turn the oven to the lowest possible temperature, close the oven door and leave the jars to heat through for 30 minutes.

Next, remove the jars from the oven or dishwasher with a towel, or from the boiling water with tongs and rubber-gloved hands; the water will evaporate from hot wet jars quite quickly. Stand the jars upright and not touching each other on a wooden board, or a bench covered with a towel to protect and insulate the bench. Pour hot (in most cases) preserves into hot jars until the jars are filled to the top (in most cases, unless indicated otherwise by the recipe). Secure the lids tightly, hold the jars firmly with a towel or an oven mitt while doing this, then leave the preserves at room temperature to cool before storing.

STORAGE

Most of the recipes say "store (preserve) in a cool dark place". In days gone by, this could have been a cool, dark corner under a house, a well-ventilated cool pantry, a corner of a garage or laundry or even a cave. The area needs to have a constant air flow and be dry, cool and dark – when a preserve is exposed to light during storage, the preserve will discolour. Anywhere dank, musty or mouldy will cause preserves to deteriorate. If the climate you live in is hot, wet and/or humid, the safest place to store preserves is in a refrigerator. If mould does develop on any preserve, throw the preserve in that particular jar away, the mould may not have developed in every jar in the same batch. The visible mould will be on the top of the preserve, but the mould will have penetrated the preserve within the jar – it is not safe to eat any food that has become mouldy during storage. Once a jar of any preserve is opened, store it in the fridge.

PECTIN

Pectin is a natural, water-soluble substance found in a variety of fruit and vegetables. When pectin is combined with sugar and acid it develops thickening properties similar to gelatine – this is most obvious in jellies and marmalades and some jams and conserves. The most common complaint made when making marmalades, conserves, jams and jellies is – "it didn't set". This can be caused by a lack of pectin in the fruit or an imbalance of pectin and acid – the pectin content of fruit is at its peak when the fruit is slightly under-ripe, that is, before the natural sugars have fully developed.

The fruits that are the best for jam-making are those that have a good balance of acid and pectin; they are usually tart or sour in taste: grapes, apples, crab apples, fresh currants, quinces, grapefruit, lemons, limes, sour oranges, plums, gooseberries and guavas.

Fruits high in pectin, but low in acid are sweet apples, guavas and quinces. It can be the type of fruit that's sweet, or fruit that's become sweet during the ripening process. To counteract this sweetness, and to increase the amount of acid, add 2 tablespoons of fresh lemon juice to each 1kg (2 pounds) of fruit used. Or, include some fruit that is low in pectin and high in acid.

Fruits low in pectin, but high in acid are pineapples, apricots, under-ripe peaches and rhubarb. To increase the pectin content, add 2 tablespoons of fresh lemon juice to each 1kg (2 pounds) of fruit used. Or, include some fruit that is high in pectin and low in acid.

Fruits low in acid and pectin are berries, melons, pears and cherries. They are not suitable to use alone in jams, and will need the addition of other fruit that contain a proper balance of acid and pectin.

JELLING

The jelling point is probably the trickiest part of jam-making to get right but, with experience, you will learn to recognise when the jelling point is reached.

The most reliable way to test if jam will jell at room temperature is to use a candy thermometer; the temperature will be marked on the thermometer, usually at 105°C/220°F.

Providing the pectin and acid levels are good, jam will jell when about half the liquid has been evaporated from the boiler. Stir the jam occasionally, but gently, towards the end of the cooking time; do this by dragging the spoon slowly across the base of the boiler, just to make sure that the jam isn't sticking, or worse – burning, on the bottom of the boiler. The flavour of burned jam is not good.

Another easy way to tell if jam will jell when it's cold is to first remove the jam from the heat, and let the bubbles subside. Dip a wooden spoon into the jam, and hold the spoon so the bowl of the spoon faces you. If the jam is ready, two or three large drops of the jam will roll along the edge of the spoon to form almost a triangle of thick jam.

If you're still in doubt, drop about a teaspoon of jam from the wooden spoon onto a chilled (in the fridge or freezer) saucer. The jam should cool quite quickly to room temperature; if the kitchen is hot, put the saucer in the fridge to hasten the cooling process. Remember, the jam should jell at room temperature, so allow for this during the testing time. Different types of jam will jell in different ways; jam can be thicker or thinner by cooking it for more or less time. Jam that is pulpy in texture, should be as spreadable as you like.

Jam with pieces of fruit suspended in it, such as marmalade, will develop a skin over the jam being tested on a saucer. Push the jam with your finger, the skin will wrinkle if the jam is ready.

If the jam is not jelling, return it to the heat and boil it again, this might only take a few minutes. If the jam refuses to set, try adding about 2 tablespoons of lemon juice, or the same amount of sherry, whisky or brandy – if you like the flavour of alcohol. Reboil the jam and test it again. If this fails, use commercial pectin (available at supermarkets and health-food stores) to set the jam. Follow the instructions on the packet.

JELLIES

Jellies are quicker and easier to make than jams, conserves and marmalades, and they're delicious. A properly-made jelly should be sparkling-clear and have a slight wobble, but still be firm enough to hold its shape when "cut" with a teaspoon. Similar rules about pectin, acid, ripeness, boiling, storing, etc, apply to jellies as well as jams.

Here is a basic method to use for fruits such as sour apples, crab apples, quince, guava and sour grapes.

1   **WASH THE FRUIT WELL**, cut away any damaged parts; chop the fruit very roughly and put it into a boiler with seeds, skins, stems, etc. This mixture should not be any deeper than 2.5 cm (1inch).

2   **ADD ENOUGH WATER** to barely cover the fruit – the fruit should just begin to float. The mixture should be about 5cm (2 inches) deep at this stage.

3   **COVER THE BOILER** with a tight-fitting lid, bring to the boil over a high heat, then reduce the heat until the mixture simmers gently. Cook, covered, until the fruit is pulpy – this could take an hour or more, depending on the type of fruit and its degree of ripeness.

4   **WHILE THE FRUIT** is cooking, prepare a cloth to strain the fruit mixture through. Use a fine cloth, such as a thoroughly soaked (if new) then washed and rinsed muslin, sheeting or unbleached calico. Jelly bags can be bought from specialty food shops, or make a jelly bag by securing the dampened cloth to the legs of an upturned stool. The cloth should sag, so that the heavy fruit mixture drips into a bowl below.

5   **POUR THE FRUIT MIXTURE** into the cloth, cover loosely with plastic to keep it clean; leave the fruit mixture to drip into the bowl for 12 hours or so. Don't squeeze or push the

successful preserving

MARMALADE
Using a large metal spoon, remove and discard any scum from the surface of the marmalade.

MARMALADE
Use a medium heatproof jug to pour the hot jam into hot sterilised jars; seal while hot. Label and date the jars when cold, and store them in a cool, dark place.

JELLING
Dip a wooden spoon into the jam, and hold the bowl of the spoon towards you. If the jam is ready, two or three large drops will roll along the edge of the spoon to form almost a triangle of thick jam.

JELLING
Drop a teaspoon of jam onto a chilled (in the fridge or freezer) saucer. The jam should cool quickly to room temperature.

fruit through the cloth, as this will cause the jelly to be cloudy.

6 **DO A QUICK PECTIN TEST** to judge how much sugar is needed for this basic recipe. Put a teaspoon of the fruit liquid into a cup or glass, and add 3 teaspoons methylated spirits. Stir the mixture gently, if it forms a fairly solid, jelly-like clot, the fruit liquid is high in pectin, in which case allow 1 cup fruit liquid to 1 cup of sugar. This means the jelly will jell quickly so, be aware that the cooking time could be as little as 10 minutes. Use a candy thermometer or the saucer test to establish if the jelly has jelled. If several smaller clots appear after stirring the methylated spirits and fruit liquid together, use ¾ cup sugar to each 1 cup of fruit liquid. If the mixture doesn't clot, or if the clots are tiny, use the lesser amount of sugar and add 2 tablespoons lemon juice to the mixture after the sugar has been

dissolved. If all else fails, resort to using a commercial pectin to set the jelly, following the packet directions. We have coloured the fruit liquid – which is usually fairly clear – to make it easier for you to see the pectin test (below).

7 **RETURN THE FRUIT LIQUID** to the boiler, it should be no more than 2.5cm (1 inch) deep; bring the liquid to the boil, uncovered. Add the sugar, stir over a high heat, without boiling, until the sugar is dissolved. Boil rapidly, uncovered – it will be foamy – without stirring, until the mixture jells when tested. Remove the jelly from the heat, allow the bubbles to subside and skim and discard any scum from the surface of the jelly.

Use a medium heatproof jug to pour the hot jelly into the hot sterilised jars. Seal the jars while hot. Label and date when cold, and store in a cool dark place.

CHUTNEYS, PICKLES, RELISHES & SAUCES

These condiments are all made from a variety of vegetables, fruits, sugar, spices and vinegar. During storage they usually mellow and improve in flavour. Their keeping qualities depend on the amount of acid (vinegar or sometimes citrus juice) and sugar used in the recipe. Most chutneys, pickles and sauces will keep for a year if they're made and stored correctly, the same as jams and jellies. Relishes, on the other hand, are often made with a variety of vegetables and fruit that are not ideal for long-term storage (that is, they are more perishable). Also, relish recipes often don't contain enough acid (vinegar/citrus juice) and sugar to preserve them; so, generally, relishes must be stored in the refrigerator and should be used within weeks, not months.

JELLING

Push the jam with your finger, the skin will wrinkle if the jam is ready. If the jam is not jelling, return it to the heat and boil it again.

JELLIES

Secure the cloth (unbleached calico or muslin) to the legs of an upturned stool. The cloth should sag, so that the heavy fruit mixture drips into a bowl below. Strain the fruit mixture through a damp cloth.

PECTIN TEST

A pectin test will tell how much sugar is needed for the basic recipe (see page 9). Stir the mixture gently, if it forms a fairly solid jelly-like clot, the fruit liquid is high in pectin.

CHUTNEYS, RELISHES

Tying various spices in a piece of muslin makes them easier to remove when the chutney (or other preserve) is ready to be poured into jars.

9

jams, marmalades and jellies

lemon curd

6 egg yolks

1 cup (220g) caster (superfine) sugar

80g (2½ ounces) unsalted butter, chopped coarsely

1 tablespoon finely grated lemon rind

⅔ cup (180ml) lemon juice

1 Whisk egg yolks and sugar in medium bowl until combined; transfer to small saucepan with remaining ingredients. Cook, stirring, over low heat, about 8 minutes or until mixture thickly coats the back of a wooden spoon. Remove from heat immediately; stir for 30 seconds.
2 Pour hot curd into hot sterilised jars; seal immediately. Label and date jars when cold.

prep + cook time 20 minutes **makes** 2 cups
nutritional count per tablespoon
4.1g total fat (2.2g saturated fat); 318kJ (76 cal); 9.4g carbohydrate; 0.9g protein; 0g fibre

notes It is important to cook the curd over a low heat to prevent curdling. If you're making curd for the first time, stir the ingredients, in a medium glass or china heatproof bowl, over a medium saucepan of simmering water. Make sure the base of the bowl does not touch the water in the pan. You will need about 4 lemons for this recipe.
Lemon curd will keep for several weeks in the refrigerator. If you prefer a completely smooth curd, you can strain the mixture (to remove the tiny pieces of lemon rind) through a fine sieve before pouring into jars.
Freeze the egg whites and use them later in friands, omelettes or in a pavlova.

serving ideas Serve on toast, scones, muffins and pikelets, or use as a sponge or tart filling.
variations You can make this recipe with almost any citrus fruit; simply replace the lemon rind and juice with the same amount of rind and juice of whatever citrus fruit you like – lime, orange, blood orange, mandarin, grapefruit and tangelo would all work well. If your oranges are very sweet, you might want to reduce the sugar to ¾ cup.

strawberry and orange conserve

strawberry and orange conserve

1.5 kg (3 pounds) strawberries, hulled

5 cups (1.1kg) white (granulated) sugar

½ cup (125ml) orange juice

2 tablespoons lemon juice

1 tablespoon finely grated orange rind

1 tablespoon orange-flavoured liqueur

1 Cook berries in large saucepan, covered, over low heat, about 5 minutes to extract some juice from the berries. Remove berries from pan with slotted spoon; set aside in medium bowl.
2 Add sugar and juices to berry juice in pan; stir over high heat, without boiling, until sugar dissolves. Bring to the boil; boil, uncovered, without stirring, about 30 minutes.
3 Return berries to pan, reduce heat; simmer, uncovered, about 20 minutes or until jam jells when tested. Remove from heat; stir in rind and liqueur.
4 Pour hot jam into hot sterilised jars; seal immediately. Label and date jars when cold.

prep + cook time 1¼ hours
makes 5 cups
nutritional count per tablespoon
0g total fat (0g saturated fat); 326kJ (78 cal); 19.4g carbohydrate; 0.4g protein; 0.6g fibre

apricot and vanilla bean jam

apricot and vanilla bean jam

1kg (2 pounds) fresh apricots, halved, seeded

1 vanilla bean, halved lengthways

1 cup (250ml) water

1kg (2 pounds) white (granulated) sugar

1 Combine apricots, vanilla bean and the water in large saucepan; bring to the boil. Reduce heat; simmer, covered, about 15 minutes or until mixture is pulpy.
2 Add sugar to pan; stir over high heat, without boiling, until sugar dissolves. Bring to the boil; boil, uncovered, without stirring, about 35 minutes or until jam jells when tested.
3 Discard vanilla bean. Pour hot jam into hot sterilised jars; seal immediately. Label and date jars when cold.

prep + cook time 55 minutes
makes 4 cups
nutritional count per tablespoon
0g total fat (0g saturated fat); 694kJ (166 cal); 43g carbohydrate; 0.1g protein; 0.4g fibre

rhubarb and ginger jam

1.5kg (3 pounds) trimmed rhubarb, chopped coarsely

1 cup (250ml) water

2 tablespoons lemon juice

7cm (3-inch) piece fresh ginger (35g), grated

4½ cups (1kg) white (granulated) sugar, approximately

½ cup (90g) finely chopped glacé ginger

1 Combine rhubarb, the water, juice and fresh ginger in large saucepan; bring to the boil. Reduce heat; simmer, covered, about 30 minutes or until mixture is pulpy.

2 Measure fruit mixture, allow ¾ cup sugar to each cup of fruit mixture. Return fruit mixture, sugar and glacé ginger to pan; stir over high heat, without boiling, until sugar dissolves. Bring to the boil; boil, uncovered, without stirring, about 30 minutes or until jam jells when tested.

3 Pour hot jam into hot sterilised jars; seal immediately. Label and date jars when cold.

prep + cook time 2 hours
makes 6 cups
nutritional count per tablespoon
0g total fat (0g saturated fat); 259kJ (62 cal); 15.3g carbohydrate; 0.3g protein; 0.5g fibre

note The rhubarb needs to be a deep red colour for this jam; under-ripe or green rhubarb will make the jam too tart in flavour.

spiced plum and port jam

spiced plum and port jam

1kg (2 pounds) plums, seeded, quartered

¼ cup (60ml) orange juice

1 cup (250ml) water

1 cinnamon stick, halved

½ teaspoon cloves

1 star anise

5 cups (1.1kg) white (granulated) sugar, approximately

½ cup (125ml) port

1 Combine plums, juice and the water in large saucepan; bring to the boil. Reduce heat; simmer, uncovered, about 15 minutes or until plums are pulpy.
2 Meanwhile, tie cinnamon, cloves and star anise in muslin.
3 Measure fruit mixture, allow 1 cup sugar to each cup of fruit mixture. Return fruit mixture, sugar, port and muslin bag to pan; stir over high heat, without boiling, until sugar dissolves. Bring to the boil; boil, uncovered, without stirring, about 35 minutes or until jam jells when tested.
4 Discard muslin bag. Pour hot jam into hot sterilised jars; seal immediately. Label and date jars when cold.

prep + cook time 55 minutes
makes 4 cups
nutritional count per tablespoon 0g total fat (0g saturated fat); 414kJ (99 cal); 24.6g carbohydrate; 0.1g protein; 0.4g fibre

blueberry and apple jam

blueberry and apple jam

1kg (2 pounds) blueberries

3 medium green-skinned apples (450g), peeled, cored, chopped finely

2 tablespoons lemon juice

4 cups (880g) white (granulated) sugar

1 Combine berries, apple and juice in large saucepan; bring to the boil. Reduce heat; simmer, uncovered, about 15 minutes or until berries are soft.
2 Add sugar to pan; stir over high heat, without boiling, until sugar dissolves. Bring to the boil; boil, uncovered, without stirring, about 20 minutes or until jam jells when tested.
3 Pour hot jam into hot sterilised jars; seal immediately. Label and date jars when cold.

prep + cook time 35 minutes
makes 5 cups
nutritional count per tablespoon 0g total fat (0g saturated fat); 284kJ (68 cal); 17.2g carbohydrate; 0.1g protein; 0.4g fibre

note Granny Smith apples are best for this recipe.

cherry jam

cherry jam

raspberry and mint jam

6 sprigs fresh mint, chopped coarsely

1kg (2 pounds) raspberries

2 tablespoons lemon juice

1kg (2 pounds) white (granulated) sugar

1 Tie mint in muslin. Combine berries, muslin bag and juice in large saucepan; cook over low heat, stirring occasionally, about 5 minutes or until berries are soft.
2 Add sugar; stir over high heat, without boiling, until sugar dissolves. Bring to the boil; boil, uncovered, without stirring, about 15 minutes or until jam jells when tested.
3 Discard muslin bag. Pour hot jam into hot sterilised jars; seal immediately. Label and date jars when cold.

prep + cook time 30 minutes
makes 5 cups
nutritional count per tablespoon
0.1g total fat (0g saturated fat); 301kJ (72 cal); 17.7g carbohydrate; 0.2g protein; 1g fibre

cherry jam

1kg (2 pounds) cherries, halved, seeded

2 medium pears (460g), peeled, cored, chopped finely

⅓ cup (80ml) lemon juice

1 cup (250ml) water

4 cups (880g) white (granulated) sugar, approximately

1 Combine cherries, pear, juice and the water in large saucepan; bring to the boil. Reduce heat; simmer, covered, about 15 minutes or until cherries are soft.
2 Measure fruit mixture; allow 1 cup sugar for each cup of fruit mixture. Return fruit mixture and sugar to pan; stir over high heat, without boiling, until sugar dissolves. Bring to the boil; boil, uncovered, without stirring, about 30 minutes or until jam jells when tested.
3 Pour hot jam into hot sterilised jars; seal immediately. Label and date jars when cold.

prep + cook time 1 hour
makes 4 cups
nutritional count per tablespoon
0g total fat (0g saturated fat); 347kJ (83 cal); 21.2g carbohydrate; 0.2g protein; 0.4g fibre

raspberry and mint jam

quince paste

6 medium quinces (2.1kg)

1½ cups (375ml) water

4 cups (880g) caster (superfine) sugar

1 Peel, quarter and core quinces; tie cores in muslin. Coarsely chop quince flesh.

2 Combine quince flesh and muslin bag with the water in large saucepan; bring to the boil. Boil, covered, about 35 minutes or until fruit is soft; discard muslin bag.

3 Strain fruit over large heatproof bowl, reserving ½ cup of the liquid; cool 10 minutes. Blend or process fruit with the reserved cooking liquid until smooth.

4 Return fruit mixture to pan with sugar; cook, stirring, over low heat, until sugar dissolves. Cook, over low heat, about 3½ hours, stirring frequently, until quince paste is very thick and deep ruby coloured.

5 Meanwhile, preheat oven to 100°C/200°F. Grease a loaf pan; line base with baking paper, extending paper 5cm (2 inches) over long sides.

6 Spread paste into pan. Bake about 1½ hours or until surface is dry to touch. Cool paste in pan. Remove from pan; wrap in baking paper, then in foil. Store in an airtight container in the refrigerator.

prep + cook time 6 hours (+ cooling) makes 5 cups
nutritional count per tablespoon 0g total fat (0g saturated fat); 59kJ (14 cal); 17.3g carbohydrate; 0.1g protein; 1.3g fibre

notes When the paste is sufficiently cooked, a wooden spoon drawn through the paste will leave a very distinct trail across the base of the pan. To dry out the paste, you can also place it in a fan-forced oven with only the fan working (no temperature set) overnight.

serving ideas It's a great accompaniment to cheese, or can be melted down and used in fruit tarts and pies. It should be cut into small slices to serve.

mango and strawberry jam

mango and strawberry jam

1kg (2 pounds) mangoes, chopped coarsely

750g (1½ pounds) strawberries, hulled, halved

1kg (2 pounds) white (granulated) sugar

½ cup (125ml) lemon juice

1 Combine ingredients in large saucepan; stir over high heat, without boiling, until sugar dissolves. Bring to the boil; boil, uncovered, without stirring, about 30 minutes or until jam jells when tested.

2 Pour hot jam into hot sterilised jars; seal immediately. Label and date jars when cold.

prep + cook time 50 minutes
makes 4 cups
nutritional count per tablespoon
0.1g total fat (0g saturated fat); 385kJ (92 cal); 23g carbohydrate; 0.4g protein; 0.6g fibre

peach, raspberry and Champagne jam

500g (1 pound) peaches, peeled, seeded, chopped finely

500g (1 pound) raspberries

1½ cups (330g) white (granulated) sugar

1 tablespoon lemon juice

½ cup (125ml) pink Champagne

1 Combine peaches, berries, sugar, juice and half the champagne in large saucepan; stir over high heat, without boiling, until sugar dissolves. Bring to the boil; boil, uncovered, without stirring, about 15 minutes or until jam jells when tested. Stir in remaining champagne.

2 Pour hot jam into hot sterilised jars; seal immediately. Label and date jars when cold.

prep + cook time 35 minutes
makes 3 cups
nutritional count per tablespoon
0.1g total fat (0g saturated fat); 196kJ (47 cal); 11g carbohydrate; 0.3g protein; 1g fibre

peach, raspberry and Champagne jam

classic fruit mince

classic fruit mince

1 cup (150g) raisins

1 cup (160g) dried currants

1 cup (160g) sultanas

¼ cup (40g) coarsely chopped blanched almonds

2 tablespoons coarsely chopped glacé cherries

1 large green-skinned apple (200g), peeled, grated coarsely

½ cup (110g) firmly packed light brown sugar

50g (1½ ounces) butter, melted

1 tablespoon each finely grated orange and lemon rind

¼ cup (60ml) orange juice

¼ cup (60ml) brandy

½ teaspoon mixed spice

1 Process dried fruit, nuts and cherries until coarsely chopped. Transfer to large bowl; stir in remaining ingredients. Cover; refrigerate at least 2 days, stirring every day.
2 Spoon fruit mince into sterilised jars; seal. Label and date jars.

prep time 20 minutes
(+ refrigeration) **makes** 3½ cups
nutritional count per tablespoon
1.6g total fat (0.7g saturated fat);
272kJ (65 cal); 11.5g carbohydrate;
0.5g protein; 0.7g fibre

notes Granny Smith apples are best for this recipe.
Fruit mince will keep for about 6 months in an airtight container in the refrigerator. The flavours will intensify the longer it is left before using.
serving ideas Use fruit mince in cakes, tarts and pies.

mandarin and dried apricot jam

mandarin and dried apricot jam

2 large mandarins (500g)

1 medium lemon (140g)

125g (4 ounces) dried apricots, chopped coarsely

3 cups (750ml) water

3 cups (660g) white (granulated) sugar, approximately

1 Using a vegetable peeler, peel rind thinly from mandarins and lemon, without removing any white pith. Shred rind finely. Discard pith and membranes from mandarins and lemon; chop flesh coarsely, discard seeds.
2 Combine fruit, apricots and the water in large saucepan; bring to the boil. Reduce heat; simmer, covered, about 30 minutes or until rind softens.

3 Measure fruit mixture, allow 1 cup sugar for each cup of fruit mixture. Return fruit mixture and sugar to pan; stir over high heat, without boiling, until sugar dissolves. Bring to the boil; boil, uncovered, without stirring, about 40 minutes or until jam jells when tested.
4 Pour hot jam into hot sterilised jars; seal immediately. Label and date jars when cold.

prep + cook time 1½ hours
makes 4 cups
nutritional count per tablespoon
0g total fat (0g saturated fat);
260kJ (62 cal); 15.6g carbohydrate;
0.2g protein; 0.5g fibre

green tomato jam

1kg (2 pounds) fresh whole figs

½ cup (125ml) orange juice

2 tablespoons lemon juice

1 vanilla bean, halved lengthways

3 cups (660g) white
(granulated) sugar

1 Cut each unpeeled fig into
eight wedges. Combine figs,
juices and vanilla bean in large
saucepan; bring to the boil. Reduce
heat; simmer, covered, about
20 minutes or until figs are soft.
2 Add sugar to pan; stir over high
heat, without boiling, until sugar
dissolves. Bring to the boil; boil,
uncovered, without stirring,
about 30 minutes or until jam jells
when tested. Discard vanilla bean.
3 Pour hot jam into hot sterilised
jars; seal immediately. Label and
date jars when cold.

prep + cook time 1 hour
makes 3 cups
nutritional count per tablespoon
0.1g total fat (0g saturated fat);
351kJ (84 cal); 20.9g carbohydrate;
0.4g protein; 0.7g fibre

notes You can use any variety of
fresh fig for this recipe. Omit the
vanilla bean for a plain fig jam.

green tomato jam

500g (1 pound) green-skinned
apples, peeled, cored, chopped
coarsely

4 medium green tomatoes
(600g), chopped coarsely

1 teaspoon ground ginger

1 cinnamon stick

1 cup (250ml) water

2½ cups (550g) white (granulated)
sugar, approximately

1 Combine apple, tomato, ginger,
cinnamon and the water in large
saucepan; bring to the boil.
Reduce heat; simmer, covered,
about 20 minutes or until fruit
is soft. Discard cinnamon.
2 Measure fruit mixture, allow
1 cup sugar to each cup of fruit
mixture. Return fruit mixture and
sugar to pan; stir over high heat,
without boiling, until sugar
dissolves. Bring to the boil; boil,
uncovered, without stirring,
about 15 minutes or until jam
jells when tested.
3 Pour hot jam into hot sterilised
jars; seal immediately. Label and
date jars when cold.

prep + cook time 1¼ hours
makes 3½ cups
nutritional count per tablespoon
0g total fat (0g saturated fat);
238kJ (57 cal); 14.4g carbohydrate;
0.2g protein; 0.3g fibre

note Granny Smith apples are
best for this recipe.

chunky fig and vanilla jam

any berry jam

banana jam

any berry jam

125g (4 ounces) blackberries

125g (4 ounces) blueberries

250g (8 ounces) raspberries

500g (1 pound) strawberries, hulled

⅓ cup (80ml) lemon juice

4 cups (880g) white (granulated) sugar

1 Stir ingredients in large saucepan over high heat, without boiling, until sugar dissolves; bring to the boil. Reduce heat; simmer, uncovered, without stirring, about 30 minutes or until jam jells when tested.
2 Pour hot jam into hot sterilised jars; seal immediately. Label and date jars when cold.

prep + cook time 40 minutes
makes 4 cups
nutritional count per tablespoon 0g total fat (0g saturated fat); 326kJ (78 cal); 19.5g carbohydrate; 0.3g protein; 0.7g fibre

note Use any combination of berries you like to collectively weigh 1kg (2 pounds).

banana jam

1.5kg (3 pounds) barely-ripe bananas, chopped coarsely

⅓ cup (80ml) lime juice

½ teaspoon ground cinnamon

½ cup (125ml) water

1 vanilla bean

4 cups (880g) white (granulated) sugar

1 Combine banana, juice, cinnamon and the water in large saucepan; split vanilla bean in half lengthways, scrape seeds into pan, discard pod. Bring to the boil; boil, covered, about 10 minutes or until banana is soft.
2 Add sugar; stir over high heat, without boiling, until sugar dissolves. Bring to the boil; boil, uncovered, about 20 minutes or until jam jells when tested.
3 Pour hot jam into hot sterilised jars; seal immediately. Label and date jars when cold.

prep + cook time 45 minutes
makes 4 cups
nutritional count per tablespoon 0g total fat (0g saturated fat); 372kJ (89 cal); 22.5g carbohydrate; 0.4g protein; 0.5g fibre

overnight three-citrus processor marmalade

1 medium grapefruit (425g), chopped coarsely

1 medium lemon (140g), chopped coarsely

2 large oranges (600g), chopped coarsely

1 litre (4 cups) water

8 cups (1.75kg) white (granulated) sugar

1 Process fruit, including rind and seeds, in batches, until chopped finely.

2 Combine fruit and the water in large saucepan; bring to the boil. Reduce heat; simmer, covered, 30 minutes. Remove from heat; stand, covered, overnight.

3 Add sugar to fruit mixture in pan; stir over high heat, without boiling, until sugar dissolves. Bring to the boil; boil, uncovered, without stirring, about 40 minutes or until marmalade jells when tested.

4 Pour hot marmalade into hot sterilised jars; seal immediately. Label and date jars when cold.

prep + cook time 1¼ hours (+ standing) **makes** 8 cups **nutritional count per tablespoon** 0g total fat (0g saturated fat); 309kJ (74 cal); 19g carbohydrate; 0.1g protein; 0.2g fibre

seville orange marmalade

seville orange marmalade

1kg (2 pounds) seville oranges

2 litres (8 cups) water

2kg (4 pounds) white (granulated) sugar, approximately

1 Slice oranges thinly, reserve seeds. Combine orange slices and the water in large saucepan; stand, covered, overnight. Place reserved seeds in small jug, barely cover with water; stand, covered, overnight.

2 Bring orange mixture to the boil. Reduce heat; simmer, covered, about 1 hour or until rind is soft.

3 Meanwhile, strain seeds, reserve liquid; discard the seeds.

4 Measure orange mixture, allow 1 cup sugar for each cup of orange mixture. Return orange mixture, sugar and reserved liquid to pan; stir over high heat, without boiling, until sugar dissolves. Bring to the boil; boil, uncovered, without stirring, about 30 minutes or until marmalade jells when tested.

5 Pour hot marmalade into hot sterilised jars; seal immediately. Label and date jars when cold.

prep + cook time 1¾ hours (+ standing) **makes** 10 cups
nutritional count per tablespoon 0g total fat (0g saturated fat); 280kJ (67 cal); 17.3g carbohydrate; 0.1g protein; 0.2g fibre

rhubarb and orange marmalade

rhubarb and orange marmalade

1kg (2 pounds) oranges

1kg (2 pounds) trimmed rhubarb, chopped coarsely

6 cups (1.3kg) white (granulated) sugar

1 Peel oranges; slice rind with pith thinly. Squeeze juice from oranges (you need 1½ cups juice).

2 Combine rind, juice, rhubarb and sugar in large saucepan; stir over high heat, without boiling, until sugar dissolves. Bring to the boil; boil, uncovered, without stirring, about 45 minutes or until marmalade jells when tested.

3 Pour hot marmalade into hot sterilised jars; seal immediately. Label and date jars when cold.

prep + cook time 1¼ hours
makes 6 cups
nutritional count per tablespoon 0g total fat (0g saturated fat); 326kJ (78 cal); 19.4g carbohydrate; 0.3g protein; 0.6g fibre

note For best results use only the reddest parts of the rhubarb stems.

cranberry and lemon marmalade

mandarin marmalade

1kg (2 pounds) mandarins

¼ cup (60ml) lemon juice

1 litre (4 cups) water

5 cups (1.1kg) white (granulated) sugar, approximately

1 Combine whole mandarins, juice and the water in large saucepan; bring to the boil. Reduce heat; simmer, covered, about 45 minutes or until fruit is soft.
2 Remove mandarins from liquid; reserve liquid. Coarsely chop mandarins, including rind; discard seeds. Return chopped mandarin to reserved liquid.
3 Measure fruit mixture, allow 1 cup sugar for each cup of fruit mixture. Return fruit mixture and sugar to pan; stir over high heat, without boiling, until sugar dissolves. Bring to the boil; boil, uncovered, without stirring, about 30 minutes or until jam jells when tested.
4 Pour hot marmalade into hot sterilised jars; seal immediately. Label and date jars when cold.

prep + cook time 1¼ hours
makes 4 cups
nutritional count per tablespoon
0g total fat (0g saturated fat); 405kJ (97 cal); 24.6g carbohydrate; 0.2g protein; 0.4g fibre

cranberry and lemon marmalade

7 medium lemons (980g)

1 litre (4 cups) water

300g (9½ ounces) fresh or frozen cranberries

5 cups (1.1kg) white (granulated) sugar

1 Halve 5 lemons, then slice thinly, reserving any seeds and juice. Juice and seed remaining lemons. Tie seeds in muslin.
2 Combine lemon slices, juice, muslin bag and the water in large saucepan, bring to the boil; boil, uncovered, about 1 hour or until rind is soft, adding cranberries for the last 20 minutes of cooking time. Discard muslin bag.
3 Add sugar to pan; stir over high heat, without boiling, until sugar dissolves. Bring to the boil; boil, uncovered, about 15 minutes or until marmalade jells when tested.
4 Pour hot marmalade into hot sterilised jars; seal immediately. Label and date jars when cold.

prep + cook time 1½ hours
makes 7 cups
nutritional count per tablespoon
0g total fat (0g saturated fat); 226kJ (54 cal); 13.4g carbohydrate; 0.1g protein; 0.4g fibre

mandarin marmalade

master orange marmalade

1kg (2 pounds) oranges

1.5 litres (6 cups) water

4½ cups (1kg) white (granulated) sugar, approximately

1 Peel oranges, removing rind and white pith separately; slice rind thinly, reserve half the pith. Quarter oranges; slice flesh thinly, reserve any seeds. Tie reserved pith and seeds in muslin.
2 Combine rind, flesh, muslin bag and the water in large saucepan; bring to the boil. Reduce heat; simmer, covered, about 1 hour or until rind is soft. Discard muslin bag.
3 Measure fruit mixture, allow 1 cup sugar for each cup of fruit mixture. Return orange mixture and sugar to pan; stir over high heat, without boiling, until sugar dissolves. Bring to the boil; boil, uncovered, without stirring, about 30 minutes or until marmalade jells when tested.
4 Pour hot marmalade into hot sterilised jars; seal immediately. Label and date jars when cold.

prep + cook time 1¾ hours
makes 4 cups
nutritional count per tablespoon
0g total fat (0g saturated fat); 368kJ (88 cal); 22.5g carbohydrate; 0.2g protein; 0.4g fibre

note This basic method of making marmalade will work with most citrus fruits including grapefruit, lemons, tangerines pomelos and limes or various combinations of these fruits.

orange, coriander and ginger marmalade

cumquat marmalade

1kg (2 pounds) cumquats

2 tablespoons lemon juice

1.25 litres (5 cups) water

6 cups (1.3kg) white (granulated) sugar

1 Quarter cumquats, being careful not to cut all the way through. Squeeze cumquats to release seeds. Tie seeds in muslin. Process cumquats until finely chopped. Combine cumquats, muslin bag, juice and the water in large saucepan; stand, covered, overnight.
2 Bring cumquat mixture to the boil. Reduce heat; simmer, covered, about 30 minutes or until rind is soft. Discard muslin bag.
3 Add sugar; stir over high heat, without boiling, until sugar dissolves. Bring to the boil; boil, uncovered, without stirring, about 30 minutes or until marmalade jells when tested.
4 Pour hot marmalade into hot sterilised jars; seal immediately. Label and date jars when cold.

prep + cook time 1½ hours (+ standing) **makes** 6 cups
nutritional count per tablespoon
0g total fat (0g saturated fat);
314kJ (75 cal); 19.2g carbohydrate;
0.1g protein; 0.3g fibre

orange, coriander and ginger marmalade

4 large oranges (1.2kg)

1 tablespoon coriander seeds, crushed

5cm (2-inch) piece fresh ginger (25g), sliced thinly

1 litre (4 cups) water

5 cups (1.1kg) white (granulated) sugar

1 Cut oranges in half. Squeeze juice; reserve juice and seeds separately. Tie reserved seeds, coriander seeds and ginger in muslin bag.
2 Using a sharp knife, remove rind as thinly as possible from orange halves; discard pith. Cut rind into thin strips.
3 Combine rind, reserved juice, muslin bag and the water in large saucepan; bring to the boil. Reduce heat; simmer, covered, about 1 hour or until rind is soft. Discard muslin bag.
4 Add sugar; stir over high heat, without boiling, until sugar dissolves. Bring to the boil; boil, uncovered, without stirring, about 40 minutes or until marmalade jells when tested.
5 Pour hot marmalade into hot sterilised jars; seal immediately. Label and date jars when cold.

prep + cook time 1¾ hours
makes 5 cups
nutritional count per tablespoon
0g total fat (0g saturated fat);
318kJ (76 cal); 19.6g carbohydrate;
0.2g protein; 0.3g fibre

note You can cut the rind into strips as thin or thick as you like; adjust the cooking time accordingly.

cumquat marmalade

thick-cut dark whisky marmalade

thick-cut dark whisky marmalade

4 large oranges (1.2kg)

2 medium lemons (280g)

1.5 litres (6 cups) water

2 cups (440g) white (granulated) sugar, approximately

2 cups (440g) firmly packed dark brown sugar, approximately

2 tablespoons treacle

2 tablespoons whisky

1 Peel oranges and lemons thickly; slice peel thickly, chop flesh coarsely. Discard seeds.

2 Combine peel, flesh and the water in large saucepan; bring to the boil. Reduce heat; simmer, covered, about 1 hour or until rind is soft.

3 Measure fruit mixture, allow ½ cup of each sugar for each cup of fruit mixture. Return fruit mixture, sugar and treacle to pan; stir over high heat, without boiling, until sugar dissolves. Bring to the boil; boil, uncovered, without stirring, about 40 minutes or until marmalade jells when tested. Stir in whisky.

4 Pour hot marmalade into hot sterilised jars; seal immediately. Label and date jars when cold.

prep + cook time 1¾ hours
makes 5 cups
nutritional count per tablespoon
0g total fat (0g saturated fat); 284kJ (68 cal); 16.7g carbohydrate; 0.3g protein; 0.5g fibre

orange and carrot marmalade

orange and carrot marmalade

2 large oranges (600g)

1 medium lemon (140g)

2 cups (500ml) water

1 large carrot (180g), grated coarsely

5 cups (1.1kg) white (granulated) sugar, approximately

1 Cut oranges and lemon in half; slice thinly, reserving seeds. Tie seeds in muslin.

2 Combine fruit, muslin bag and the water in large saucepan; bring to the boil. Reduce heat; simmer, covered, 45 minutes. Add carrot; simmer, covered, about 15 minutes or until rind is soft. Discard muslin bag.

3 Measure fruit mixture, allow ¾ cup sugar for each cup of fruit mixture. Return fruit mixture and sugar to pan; stir over high heat, without boiling, until sugar dissolves. Bring to the boil; boil, uncovered, without stirring, about 40 minutes or until marmalade jells when tested.

4 Pour hot marmalade into hot sterilised jars; seal immediately. Label and date jars when cold.

prep + cook time 1¾ hours
makes 4 cups
nutritional count per tablespoon
0g total fat (0g saturated fat); 397kJ (95 cal); 24.1g carbohydrate; 0.2g protein; 0.4g fibre

mint jelly

1kg (2 pounds) green-skinned apples, unpeeled, chopped coarsely

1.5 litres (6 cups) water

5½ cups (1.2kg) white (granulated) sugar, approximately

green food colouring

1 cup firmly packed fresh mint leaves

1 Combine apple and the water in large saucepan; bring to the boil. Reduce heat; simmer, covered, about 1 hour or until apple is pulpy.

2 Strain mixture through a fine cloth into large bowl. Stand 3 hours or overnight until liquid stops dripping. Do not squeeze cloth; discard pulp.

3 Measure apple liquid; allow 1 cup sugar for each cup of liquid. Return apple liquid and sugar to same pan; stir over high heat, without boiling, until sugar dissolves. Bring to the boil; boil rapidly, uncovered, without stirring, about 30 minutes or until jelly jells when tested.

4 Pour jelly into large heatproof jug; stir in a little food colouring. Stand until jelly is lukewarm (but not set).

5 Meanwhile, drop mint into small saucepan of boiling water for 2 seconds; drain. Rinse under cold water; drain, pat dry with absorbent paper. Chop mint finely; stir into lukewarm jelly.

6 Pour jelly into hot sterilised jars; seal immediately. Label and date jars when cold.

prep + cook time 2 hours (+ standing) **makes** 6 cups **nutritional count per tablespoon** 0g total fat (0g saturated fat); 288kJ (69 cal); 17.9g carbohydrate; 0.1g protein; 0.2g fibre

notes Granny Smith apples are best for this recipe.
Store mint jelly in a cool, dark place for 3 months. Refrigerate after opening. The jelly has a natural soft pink colour before the colouring is used, you might prefer to omit the colouring.
serving ideas Serve with roast lamb, barbecued cutlets or chops.

apple and passionfruit jelly

1kg (2 pounds) green-skinned apples, unpeeled, chopped coarsely

¾ cup (180ml) passionfruit pulp

1.5 litres (6 cups) water

5 cups (1.1kg) white (granulated) sugar, approximately

1 Combine apple, pulp and the water in large saucepan; bring to the boil. Reduce heat; simmer, covered, about 1 hour or until mixture is pulpy.
2 Strain mixture through a fine cloth into large bowl. Stand 3 hours or overnight until liquid stops dripping. Do not squeeze cloth; discard pulp.
3 Measure apple liquid, allow 1 cup sugar for each cup of liquid. Return apple liquid and sugar to pan; stir over high heat, without boiling, until sugar dissolves. Bring to the boil; boil rapidly, uncovered, without stirring, about 20 minutes or until jelly jells when tested.
4 Pour hot jelly into hot sterilised jars; seal immediately. Label and date jars when cold.

prep + cook time 1¾ hours (+ standing) **makes** 5 cups
nutritional count per tablespoon 0g total fat (0g saturated fat); 330kJ (59 cal); 20g carbohydrate; 0.1g protein; 0.7g fibre

notes Granny Smith apples are best for this recipe. You will need about 10 passionfruit.

apple jelly

apple jelly

1kg (2 pounds) green-skinned apples, unpeeled, chopped coarsely

1.5 litres (6 cups) water

6 cups (1.3kg) white (granulated) sugar, approximately

1 Combine apple, including core and seeds, and the water in large saucepan; bring to the boil. Reduce heat; simmer, covered, about 1 hour or until pulpy.
2 Strain mixture through a fine cloth into large bowl. Stand 3 hours or overnight until liquid stops dripping. Do not squeeze cloth; discard pulp.
3 Measure apple liquid, allow 1 cup sugar for each cup of liquid. Return apple liquid and sugar to pan; stir over high heat, without boiling, until sugar dissolves. Bring to the boil; boil rapidly, uncovered, without stirring, about 20 minutes or until jelly jells when tested.
4 Pour hot jelly into hot sterilised jars; seal immediately. Label and date jars when cold.

prep + cook time 1¾ hours (+ standing) **makes** 5 cups
nutritional count per tablespoon 0g total fat (0g saturated fat); 372kJ (89 cal); 23.1g carbohydrate; 0g protein; 0.3g fibre

notes Granny Smith apples are best for this recipe. This is a good base jelly – for slight variations try adding cinnamon sticks, rosemary sprigs or dried lavender to the jelly.

grape jelly

2kg (4 pounds) black grapes

⅓ cup (80ml) lemon juice

⅔ cup (160ml) water

3¾ cups (825g) white
(granulated) sugar

50g (1½ ounces) powdered
pectin (jamsetta)

1 Remove grapes from main
thick stems, leaving small stems
attached to grapes; place in large
saucepan. Crush grapes lightly
with a potato masher or fork.
Add juice and the water; bring
to the boil. Reduce heat; simmer,
covered, about 25 minutes or
until mixture is pulpy.
2 Strain mixture through a fine
cloth into large bowl. Stand
3 hours or overnight until liquid
stops dripping. Do not squeeze
cloth; discard pulp.
3 Return grape liquid to pan
with sugar; stir over high heat,
without boiling, until sugar
dissolves. Bring to the boil; boil,
uncovered, without stirring,
15 minutes. Sprinkle pectin over
jelly; boil rapidly, uncovered,
without stirring, about 5 minutes
or until jelly jells when tested.
4 Pour hot jelly into hot sterilised
jars; seal immediately. Label and
date jars when cold.

prep + cook time 1 hour
(+ standing) **makes** 5 cups
nutritional count per tablespoon
0g total fat (0g saturated fat);
268kJ (64 cal); 16.3g carbohydrate;
0.2g protein; 0.2g fibre

chutneys, pickles and relishes

beetroot chutney

6 medium fresh beetroot (beets) (1kg), trimmed

2 teaspoons cumin seeds

1 cinnamon stick, broken

4 cardamom pods, bruised

4 large green-skinned apples (800g), peeled, cored, chopped coarsely

1 medium red onion (170g), chopped coarsely

2 cloves garlic, crushed

2cm (¾-inch) piece fresh ginger (10g) grated

1 cup (220g) white (granulated) sugar

2 cups (500ml) white vinegar

2 tablespoons lemon juice

1 teaspoon coarse cooking salt (kosher salt)

1 Boil, steam or microwave beetroot until tender; drain. When cool enough to handle, peel beetroot. Finely chop half the beetroot; blend or process remaining beetroot until smooth.
2 Tie spices in muslin. Combine pureed beetroot and muslin bag with apple, onion, garlic, ginger, sugar, vinegar, juice and salt in large saucepan; stir over high heat, without boiling, until sugar dissolves. Bring to the boil. Reduce heat; simmer, uncovered, stirring occasionally, 30 minutes. Add chopped beetroot; simmer, uncovered, about 10 minutes or until chutney is thick. Discard muslin bag.
3 Spoon hot chutney into hot sterilised jars; seal immediately. Label and date jars when cold.

prep + cook time 1¼ hours **makes** 6 cups
nutritional count per tablespoon
0g total fat (0g saturated fat);
96kJ (23 cal); 5.1g carbohydrate;
0.3g protein; 0.6g fibre

notes Granny Smith apples are best for this recipe. Store chutney in a cool, dark place for at least three weeks before opening. Wear disposable gloves when peeling beetroot as it does stain hands. Refrigerate after opening.
serving ideas Serve with roast beef and pork or on steak sandwiches and burgers.

green tomato chutney

2kg (4 pounds) green tomatoes, cored, chopped coarsely

2 large brown onions (400g), chopped coarsely

2 large green-skinned apples (400g), peeled, cored, chopped coarsely

2 cups (440g) raw sugar

2½ cups (625ml) cider vinegar

1 cup (150g) sultanas

4 fresh long red chillies, chopped finely

6 cloves garlic, chopped finely

2 teaspoons coarse cooking salt (kosher salt)

1 Stir ingredients in large saucepan over high heat, without boiling, until sugar dissolves; bring to the boil. Reduce heat; simmer, uncovered, stirring occasionally, about 1½ hours or until chutney is thick.

2 Spoon hot chutney into hot sterilised jars; seal immediately. Label and date jars when cold.

prep + cook time 2 hours
makes 5 cups
nutritional count per tablespoon
0.1g total fat (0g saturated fat); 201kJ (48 cal); 10.8g carbohydrate; 0.5g protein; 0.8g fibre

notes Granny Smith apples are best for this recipe.
Store chutney in a cool, dark place for at least three weeks before opening. Refrigerate after opening. This recipe is quite spicy; for a milder version you can remove the seeds from the chillies or use less chilli.
serving ideas Serve with cold meats and cheese or on sandwiches and burgers.

green mango chutney

4 green mangoes (1.4kg), chopped coarsely

1 medium brown onion (150g), chopped finely

1¼ cups (275g) firmly packed light brown sugar

2 cups (500ml) white vinegar

2 teaspoons garam masala

3cm (1¼-inch) piece fresh ginger (15g), grated

1 teaspoon coarse cooking salt (kosher salt)

1 Stir ingredients in large saucepan over high heat, without boiling, until sugar dissolves; bring to the boil. Reduce heat; simmer, uncovered, stirring occasionally, about 45 minutes or until chutney is thick.

2 Spoon hot chutney into hot sterilised jars; seal immediately. Label and date jars when cold.

prep + cook time 1¼ hours
makes 3½ cups
nutritional count per tablespoon
0.1g total fat (0g saturated fat); 171kJ (41 cal); 9.4g carbohydrate; 0.3g protein; 0.4g fibre

notes Store chutney in a cool, dark place for at least three weeks before opening. Refrigerate after opening.
serving ideas Serve with curries, tandoori chicken and lamb skewers.

watermelon rind chutney

2kg (4 pound) piece watermelon

1½ cups (375ml) white wine vinegar

1 cup (250ml) water

1½ cups (330g) white (granulated) sugar

5cm (2-inch) piece fresh ginger (25g), grated

2 teaspoons black peppercorns

2 fresh small red thai (serrano) chillies, sliced thinly

1 Remove pink flesh from watermelon; reserve for another use. Carefully remove and discard green skin from the white rind; cut white rind into 2cm (¾-inch) pieces.
2 Stir white rind and remaining ingredients in large saucepan over high heat, without boiling, until sugar dissolves. Bring to the boil. Reduce heat; simmer, uncovered, stirring occasionally, about 1 hour or until mixture is syrupy and rind is translucent and tender.
3 Spoon hot chutney into hot sterilised jars; seal immediately. Label and date jars when cold.

prep + cook time 1½ hours
makes 2 cups
nutritional count per tablespoon 0g total fat (0g saturated fat); 247kJ (59 cal); 14.5g carbohydrate; 0g protein; 0.1g fibre

notes Granny Smith apples are best for this recipe. Store chutney in a cool, dark place for at least three weeks before opening. Refrigerate after opening.
serving ideas Serve with Asian-style barbecued meats or cheese.

mango chutney

3 medium mangoes (1.3kg), chopped coarsely

1 cup (150g) coarsely chopped dried apricots

2 medium red onions (340g), chopped finely

1½ cups (330g) firmly packed light brown sugar

2 cups (500ml) cider vinegar

6 cloves garlic, chopped finely

1 teaspoon ground ginger

½ teaspoon dried chilli flakes

1 teaspoon coarse cooking salt (kosher salt)

1 Stir ingredients in large saucepan over high heat, without boiling, until sugar dissolves; bring to the boil. Reduce heat; simmer, uncovered, stirring occasionally, about 1 hour or until chutney is thick.

2 Spoon hot chutney into hot sterilised jars; seal immediately. Label and date jars when cold.

prep + cook time 1¼ hours
makes 4 cups
nutritional count per tablespoon 0.1g total fat (0g saturated fat); 196kJ (47cal); 10.7g carbohydrate; 0.5g protein; 0.7g fibre

note Store chutney in a cool, dark place for at least three weeks before opening. Refrigerate after opening.
serving ideas Serve with grilled meats, fish and curries.

sweet fruit chutney

1kg (2 pounds) green-skinned apples, peeled, cored, chopped coarsely

800g (1½ pounds) tomatoes, peeled, chopped coarsely

2 large brown onions (400g), chopped coarsely

1 cup (150g) coarsely chopped dried apricots

1 cup (140g) coarsely chopped seeded dried dates

1 cup (160g) dried currants

2cm (¾-inch) piece fresh ginger (10g), grated

2½ cups (625ml) malt vinegar

2 cups (440g) firmly packed light brown sugar

2 teaspoons mixed spice

¼ teaspoon cayenne pepper

1 tablespoon coarse cooking salt (kosher salt)

1 Stir ingredients in large saucepan over high heat, without boiling, until sugar dissolves; bring to the boil. Reduce heat; simmer, uncovered, stirring occasionally, about 1½ hours or until chutney is thick.

2 Spoon hot chutney into hot sterilised jars; seal immediately. Label and date jars when cold.

prep + cook time 2 hours
makes 9 cups
nutritional count per tablespoon
0g total fat (0g saturated fat); 138kJ (33 cal); 7.5g carbohydrate; 0.3g protein; 0.6g fibre

notes Granny Smith apples are best for this recipe.
Store chutney in a cool, dark place for at least three weeks before opening. Refrigerate after opening.
serving ideas Serve chutney with cold meats and cheese or on sandwiches.

Depending on the ripeness of the peaches, peel them using a vegetable peeler or, blanch them by cutting a small cross in the base of each peach; cover with boiling water in a heatproof bowl. Stand 5 minutes, then transfer peaches to a bowl of iced water. Using fingers or a small knife, carefully remove the skin.

peach and ginger chutney

1.8kg (3½ pounds) peaches (almost ripe), peeled, chopped coarsely

1 cup (150g) raisins

1 large red onion (300g), chopped coarsely

1½ cups (330g) white (granulated) sugar

2 cups (500ml) cider vinegar

8cm (3¼-inch) piece fresh ginger (40g), grated

2 fresh long red chillies, halved, sliced thinly

1 cinnamon stick

1 teaspoon coarse cooking salt (kosher salt)

1 Stir ingredients in large saucepan over high heat, without boiling, until sugar dissolves; bring to the boil. Reduce heat; simmer, uncovered, stirring occasionally, about 1¼ hours or until chutney is thick. Discard cinnamon stick.

2 Spoon hot chutney into hot sterilised jars; seal immediately. Label and date jars when cold.

prep + cook time 2 hours
makes 5½ cups
nutritional count per tablespoon
0g total fat (0g saturated fat); 150kJ (36 cal); 8.4g carbohydrate; 0.3g protein; 0.5g fibre

note Store chutney in a cool, dark place for at least three weeks before opening. Refrigerate after opening.
serving ideas Serve with cold meats, cheese, chicken, pork or on burgers.

chilli jam

1kg (2 pounds) ripe egg (plum) tomatoes, chopped coarsely

2¼ cups (500g) caster (superfine) sugar

⅓ cup (80ml) white vinegar

¼ cup (60ml) lemon juice

6 fresh long red chillies, sliced thinly

2 fresh small red thai (serrano) chillies, sliced thinly

4cm (1½-inch) piece fresh ginger (20g), grated

3 cloves garlic, crushed

2 tablespoons fish sauce

1 teaspoon coarse cooking salt (kosher salt)

1 Stir ingredients in large saucepan over high heat, without boiling, until sugar dissolves. Bring to the boil. Reduce heat; simmer, uncovered, stirring occasionally, about 1¼ hours or until jam is thick. Cool 15 minutes.
2 Blend or process chilli mixture, in batches, until smooth. Pour into hot sterilised jars; seal immediately. Label and date jars when cold.

prep + cook time 1¾ hours (+ cooling) **makes** 3⅓ cups
nutritional count per tablespoon 0g total fat (0g saturated fat); 226kJ (54 cal); 13.1g carbohydrate; 0.4g protein; 0.4g fibre

notes Store in a cool, dark place for up to three months. Refrigerate after opening. Wear plastic disposable gloves when cutting chillies as they can burn your skin.

serving ideas Use in stir-fries, marinades and sauces; use sparingly, as it is very hot.

indian tamarind chutney

375g (12 ounces) dried tamarind, chopped coarsely

3 cups (750ml) boiling water

¼ cup (55g) firmly packed light brown sugar

½ teaspoon ground turmeric

1 teaspoon coarse cooking salt (kosher salt)

5 dried kashmiri chillies, stems removed

½ cup (40g) coriander seeds

1 teaspoon cumin seeds

1 teaspoon fenugreek seeds

½ teaspoon brown mustard seeds

1 teaspoon black peppercorns

2 tablespoons vegetable oil

1 Combine tamarind and the boiling water in large heatproof bowl; stand 15 minutes. Push tamarind mixture through fine sieve into large saucepan; discard solids.
2 Add sugar, turmeric and salt to pan with tamarind mixture; stir over high heat, without boiling, until sugar dissolves. Bring to the boil. Reduce heat; simmer, uncovered, about 1 hour or until mixture is thick. Cool 15 minutes.
3 Meanwhile, blend or process chillies, seeds and peppercorns until a fine powder. Heat oil in large frying pan; cook spice mixture, stirring, about 2 minutes or until fragrant.
4 Blend or process spice mixture with tamarind mixture until smooth. Spoon chutney into hot sterilised jars; seal immediately. Label and date jars when cold.

prep + cook time 1¾ hours (+ standing & cooling)
makes 1½ cups
nutritional count per tablespoon
2g total fat (0.3g saturated fat); 142kJ (34 cal); 4g carbohydrate; 0g protein; 0g fibre

notes Store chutney in the refrigerator. This chutney is very intense, so use sparingly. Kashmiri chillies are dried long red chillies, popular in Indian cooking due to the vibrant red colour they provide to dishes.
serving ideas Serve with Indian curries and samosas.

oven-dried tomatoes

1kg (2 pounds) ripe egg (plum) tomatoes, halved lengthways

2 teaspoons coarse cooking salt (kosher salt)

½ teaspoon dried oregano

1½ cups (375ml) olive oil

1 Preheat oven to 80°C/175°F.
2 Using a small sharp knife, score cut-sides of tomatoes lengthways, without cutting through the skin; push flesh outwards. Combine tomatoes, salt and oregano in large bowl; toss gently. Stand 10 minutes.
3 Place tomatoes, in a single layer, cut-side down, on an oiled wire rack, over large oven tray. Roast, uncovered, about 15 hours or until tomatoes are dry to touch.
4 Cool tomatoes on wire rack; pack into sterilised jars. Pour enough oil into jars to cover tomatoes; seal immediately. Label and date jars.

prep + cook time 15½ hours (+ cooling) **makes** about 26 pieces
nutritional count per piece 0.8g total fat (0.1g saturated fat); 54kJ (13 cal); 0.7g carbohydrate; 0.4g protein; 0.5g fibre

notes Tomatoes will keep, refrigerated, for up to 2 weeks; or freeze them in single layers, between sheets of baking paper, in an airtight container for up to three months. Egg tomatoes are perfect for this recipe as they don't have many seeds; choose ripe unblemished tomatoes.

serving ideas Oven-dried tomatoes are delicious served on their own or as part of an antipasto platter. Use them in salads, pasta dishes, dips, frittatas and quiches.

A ploughman's lunch is a hearty, cold lunch for the labourer, usually consisting of thick slices of crusty bread, cheese, pickles and pickled onions, but this can vary considerably. It may also contain a selection of cold meats.

ploughman's pickle

¾ cup (215g) coarse cooking salt (kosher salt)

2 cups (500ml) boiling water

1.75 litres (7 cups) cold water

2 large brown onions (400g), chopped finely

1 small cauliflower (1kg), cut into small florets

5 large zucchini (750g), chopped finely

2 stalks celery (300g), trimmed, chopped finely

2 large green-skinned apples (400g), peeled, cored, chopped coarsely

3 cloves garlic, crushed

1 litre (4 cups) malt vinegar

⅓ cup (50g) cornflour (cornstarch)

3 cups (660g) firmly packed light brown sugar

3 teaspoons ground turmeric

2 teaspoons each ground cinnamon and cumin

½ teaspoon each ground nutmeg, allspice and cayenne pepper

1 Combine salt and the boiling water in large non-metallic bowl; stir until salt dissolves. Stir in the cold water. Add onion, cauliflower, zucchini and celery; stand mixture overnight.

2 Rinse and drain vegetable mixture well; drain vegetables on absorbent paper.

3 Combine apple, garlic and 2½ cups of the vinegar in large saucepan; bring to the boil. Reduce heat; simmer, uncovered, about 10 minutes or until apple is soft. Remove from heat.

4 Blend cornflour with ¼ cup of the vinegar in small jug until smooth. Add remaining vinegar, sugar and spices to pan; stir over high heat, without boiling, until sugar dissolves. Stir in cornflour mixture; cook, stirring, until mixture boils and thickens. Add vegetables; simmer, uncovered, about 5 minutes or until vegetables are tender.

5 Spoon hot pickle into hot sterilised jars; seal immediately. Label and date jars when cold.

prep + cook time 1 hour (+ standing) **makes** 10 cups
nutritional count per tablespoon
0g total fat (0g saturated fat); 113kJ (27 cal); 6.5g carbohydrate; 0.3g protein; 0.4g fibre

notes Granny Smith apples are best for this recipe.
Store pickle in a cool, dark place for at least three weeks before opening. Refrigerate after opening.
serving ideas Serve as part of a ploughman's lunch.

piccalilli

400g (12½ ounces) small pickling onions, peeled

½ cup (140g) coarse cooking salt (kosher salt)

2 cups (500ml) boiling water

1.75 litres (7 cups) cold water

1 small cauliflower (1kg), cut into small florets

250g (8 ounces) green beans, trimmed, chopped coarsely

2 medium carrots (240g), chopped coarsely

1 cup (220g) white (granulated) sugar

⅓ cup (50g) plain (all-purpose) flour

2 tablespoons mustard powder

2 teaspoons ground turmeric

½ teaspoon cayenne pepper

1 litre (4 cups) cider vinegar

1 Peel onions, leaving a tiny part of the roots intact to hold the onions together. Combine salt and the boiling water in large non-metallic heatproof bowl; stir until salt dissolves. Add the cold water. Add vegetables; mix well. Cover with a large plate or a sealed plastic bag half-filled with water to keep vegetables submerged; stand overnight.
2 Rinse and drain vegetables well; drain on absorbent paper.
3 Combine sugar, flour and spices in large saucepan; gradually whisk in vinegar until smooth. Cook, stirring, until mixture boils and thickens. Add vegetables; simmer, uncovered, about 10 minutes or until vegetables are barely tender.
4 Spoon hot piccalilli into hot sterilised jars; seal immediately. Label and date jars when cold.

prep + cook time 30 minutes (+ standing) **makes** 10 cups
nutritional count per tablespoon 0g total fat (0g saturated fat); 59kJ (14 cal); 2.6g carbohydrate; 0.3g protein; 0.3g fibre

note Store piccalilli in a cool, dark place for at least three weeks before opening. Refrigerate after opening.
serving ideas Serve as part of a ploughman's lunch – a cold lunch consisting of thick crusty bread, cold meats, cheese and pickles.

chow chow

500g (1 pound) cauliflower, cut into small florets

2 lebanese cucumbers (260g), unpeeled, seeded, chopped coarsely

2 cups (160g) finely shredded cabbage

300g (9½ ounces) green beans, trimmed, chopped coarsely

1 medium red capsicum (bell pepper) (200g), chopped coarsely

1 medium green capsicum (bell pepper) (200g), chopped coarsely

3½ cups (875ml) cider vinegar

1½ cups (330g) white (granulated) sugar

2 tablespoons mustard powder

1 tablespoon mustard seeds

1 teaspoon ground turmeric

pinch cayenne pepper

1 teaspoon coarse cooking salt (kosher salt)

½ cup (75g) plain (all-purpose) flour

¼ cup (60ml) water

420g (13½ ounces) canned corn kernels, drained

1 Boil, steam or microwave cauliflower, cucumber, cabbage, beans and capsicum, separately, until barely tender; drain. Transfer vegetables, as they're cooked, to a large bowl of iced water.

2 Combine vinegar, sugar, spices and salt in large saucepan; stir over high heat, without boiling, until sugar dissolves. Blend flour with the water in small jug until smooth, add to pan; cook, stirring, until mixture boils and thickens. Add drained vegetables and corn; simmer, uncovered, stirring occasionally, 5 minutes.

3 Spoon hot pickle into hot sterilised jars; seal immediately. Label and date jars when cold.

prep + cook time 1 hour
makes 8 cups
nutritional count per tablespoon
0.1g total fat (0g saturated fat); 100kJ (24 cal); 5g carbohydrate; 0.5g protein; 0.4g fibre

note Store pickle in a cool, dark place for at least one month before opening. Refrigerate after opening.

serving ideas Serve as part of a ploughman's lunch or with cold meats and cheese.

bread and butter pickle

500g (1 pound) unpeeled lebanese cucumbers, sliced thinly lengthways

1 large brown onion (200g), sliced thinly

¼ cup (70g) coarse cooking salt (kosher salt)

1 cup (250ml) white vinegar

1 cup (220g) white (granulated) sugar

2 teaspoons mustard seeds

½ teaspoon dried chilli flakes

¼ teaspoon ground turmeric

1 Combine cucumber and onion in medium non-metallic bowl; sprinkle with salt, mix well. Cover; stand overnight.

2 Rinse and drain cucumber mixture; drain on absorbent paper. Spoon into hot sterilised jars.

3 Meanwhile, stir remaining ingredients in medium saucepan over high heat, without boiling, until sugar dissolves. Bring to the boil; remove from heat. Pour enough vinegar mixture into jars to cover cucumber mixture; seal immediately. Label and date jars when cold.

prep + cook time 30 minutes (+ standing) **makes** 4 cups
nutritional count per tablespoon 0g total fat (0g saturated fat); 88kJ (21 cal); 5g carbohydrate; 0.1g protein; 0.2g fibre

notes Store pickle in a cool, dark place for at least three weeks before opening. Refrigerate after opening. The cucumbers will lose their colour on standing.
serving ideas Serve on hot dogs, hamburgers and sandwiches.

pickled chillies

250g (8 ounces) fresh long green chillies

250g (8 ounces) fresh long red chillies

3 cups (750ml) white vinegar

1½ cups (375ml) water

⅓ cup (75g) white (granulated) sugar

1½ tablespoons coarse cooking salt (kosher salt)

4 dried bay leaves

3 teaspoons peppercorn medley

3 teaspoons coriander seeds

1 Cook whole chillies in medium saucepan of boiling water until barely tender; drain. Transfer chillies to medium bowl filled with iced water. Prick chillies with a pin, about 5 times on each side; pack into hot sterilised jars.

2 Combine remaining ingredients in large saucepan; stir over high heat, without boiling, until sugar dissolves. Bring to the boil; remove from heat. Pour enough vinegar mixture into jars to cover chillies; seal immediately. Label and date jars when cold.

prep + cook time 20 minutes
makes 6 cups (about 20 chillies)
nutritional count per chilli
0.1g total fat (0g saturated fat); 113kJ (27 cal); 4.4g carbohydrate; 0.6g protein; 1.9g fibre

notes Red chillies are much spicier and hotter than green; you can use one or the other, if you prefer.
Store pickle in a cool, dark place for at least three weeks before opening. Refrigerate after opening.

serving ideas Serve with antipasto, or use slices stirred through stir-fries as you would fresh chillies.

sweet mustard pickles

½ cup (140g) coarse cooking salt (kosher salt)

2 cups (500ml) boiling water

1 litre (4 cups) cold water

500g (1 pound) cauliflower, chopped coarsely

4 medium brown onions (600g), chopped coarsely

2 lebanese cucumbers (260g), unpeeled, chopped coarsely

3 cups (750ml) cider vinegar

2 cups (440g) white (granulated) sugar

1 tablespoon mustard powder

1 teaspoon curry powder

1 teaspoon turmeric

⅓ cup (50g) cornflour (cornstarch)

2 tablespoons water

1 Combine salt and the boiling water in large non-metallic bowl; stir until salt dissolves. Add the cold water. Add vegetables; mix well. Cover with a large plate or a sealed plastic bag half-filled with water to keep vegetables submerged; stand overnight.
2 Rinse and drain vegetables well; drain on absorbent paper.
3 Combine vegetables, vinegar, sugar and spices in large saucepan; stir over high heat, without boiling, until sugar dissolves. Bring to the boil. Reduce heat; simmer, uncovered, about 10 minutes or until vegetables are tender.
4 Blend cornflour with the water in small jug until smooth, add to pan; cook, stirring, until mixture boils and thickens.
5 Spoon hot pickle into hot sterilised jars; seal immediately. Label and date jars when cold.

prep + cook time 45 minutes (+ standing) **makes** 9 cups
nutritional count per tablespoon 0g total fat (0g saturated fat); 84kJ (20 cal); 4.9g carbohydrate; 0.2g protein; 0.2g fibre

note Store pickle in a cool, dark place for at least three weeks before opening. Refrigerate after opening.
serving ideas Serve with cold meats, burgers and sausages or on ham sandwiches.

preserved lemons

8 medium lemons (1.1kg)

1½ cups (450g) rock salt

5 fresh bay leaves

1 teaspoon coriander seeds

1 teaspoon caraway seeds

1 cup (250ml) lemon juice

1 Halve lemons lengthways; carefully cut each lemon half in half again, without cutting all the way through. Open lemon halves out slightly.

2 Squeeze lemons over a large non-metallic bowl to catch the juice; add lemons to bowl with salt, bay leaves and seeds, mix well.

3 Pack lemon mixture into 1.5-litre (6-cup) sterilised jar; pour enough of the juice into the jar to cover lemons. Place a sealed small plastic bag filled with water on top of the lemons to keep them submerged; seal jar. Label and date jar.

prep time 20 minutes
makes 16 pieces
nutritional count per piece
0.1g total fat (0.1g saturated fat); 88kJ (21 cal); 1.8g carbohydrate; 0.4g protein; 1.6g fibre

notes Store preserved lemons in a cool, dark place for at least three weeks before using. Refrigerate after opening. To use, remove and discard pulp, squeeze juice from rind, rinse rind well, then slice according to the recipe. Cinnamon sticks or chillies can be added to the preserved lemons in step 2.
serving ideas Use the rinsed preserved lemon rind in tagines, couscous, salads, sauces, stews and pilafs.

cracked olives

5kg (10 pounds) green olives

2 tablespoons coarse cooking salt (kosher salt)

2 cloves garlic, crushed

1 teaspoon dried chilli flakes

2 teaspoons dried mixed herbs

4 litres (16 cups) olive oil, approximately

1 Using a small hammer, or the flat side of a meat mallet, carefully crack, but do not seed, each olive on a kitchen board. Place olives in large non-metallic bowl, plastic tub or bucket; cover with cold water. Cover with a large plate or a sealed plastic bag filled with water to keep olives submerged. Stand 12 to 16 days, changing the water every day, until olives become dark and tender. Drain.

2 Combine drained olives, salt, garlic, chilli and herbs in large strainer; stand in sink overnight. (Do not rinse olives.)

3 Spoon olives into sterilised jars; pour in enough olive oil to cover olives. Label and date jars.

prep + cook time 1½ hours (+ standing) **makes** about 25 cups (3kg/6 pounds) drained olives
nutritional count per ¼ cup 2.2g total fat (0.3g saturated fat); 88kJ (21 cal); 0.4g carbohydrate; 0.2g protein; 0.4g fibre

notes You must use fresh, raw green olives, not those from the deli, as these have already been brined. Green olives range from light green to a mottled dark olive green colour; these are all fine to use. Olives have a short season, and are usually available during autumn.

Store in a cool, dark place for at least two weeks before opening. Olives will keep for up to 12 months; refrigerate after opening.

The amount of olive oil you will need depends on the size and shape of the jars used. Pack olives tightly into the jar but be gentle to avoid bruising.

Olives may float to the surface; to keep them submerged, place a slice of lemon or a sealed small plastic bag filled with water on top of the olives before closing the jars.

You can change the flavourings of marinated olives to suit your taste. Try adding sprigs of thyme, rosemary or dried oregano, strips of lemon or orange rind, bay leaves, peppercorns, sun-dried tomatoes or mustard seeds.

Warn anyone eating these olives that they still contain the seed.

serving idea Serve with antipasto.

pickled onions

1kg (2 pounds) small pickling onions

½ cup (140g) coarse cooking salt (kosher salt)

1 cup (250ml) boiling water

2 cups (250ml) cold water

2 fresh long red chillies, halved lengthways

3 cups (750ml) white wine vinegar

1 cup (250ml) white vinegar

¾ cup (165g) raw sugar

2 dried bay leaves

1 tablespoon black peppercorns

1 Place onions in large heatproof non-metallic bowl, cover with boiling water; stand 5 minutes, drain. Peel onions, leaving a tiny part of the roots intact to hold the onions together; return to bowl.
2 Combine salt and the boiling water in large heatproof jug; stir until salt dissolves. Add the cold water; pour over onions. Cover with a large plate or a sealed plastic bag half-filled with water to keep onions submerged; stand overnight.
3 Rinse and drain onions; pat onions dry with absorbent paper. Pack onions and chilli into hot sterilised jars.
4 Stir remaining ingredients in medium saucepan over high heat, without boiling, until sugar dissolves. Bring to the boil; remove from heat. Pour enough vinegar mixture into jars to cover onions; seal immediately. Label and date jars when cold.

prep + cook time 45 minutes (+ standing) **makes** 6 cups
nutritional count per ¼ cup
0g total fat (0g saturated fat); 192kJ (46 cal); 9.1g carbohydrate; 0.6g protein; 0.6g fibre

note Store pickle in a cool, dark place for at least three weeks before opening. Refrigerate after opening.
serving ideas Serve with cold meats, antipasto and cheese.

garlic confit

onion jam

garlic confit

7 medium garlic bulbs (500g),
cloves separated, unpeeled

1 dried bay leaf

2 cups (500ml) olive oil,
approximately

1 Preheat oven to 150°C/300°F.
2 Place garlic and bay leaf in
small baking dish; add enough
oil to dish to cover garlic. Roast,
uncovered, about 45 minutes or
until garlic is soft.
3 Spoon garlic and bay leaf
into sterilised jars. Carefully
pour enough of the oil left in
dish into jars to cover garlic;
seal immediately. Label and
date jars when cold.

prep + cook time 50 minutes
makes 4 cups
nutritional count per tablespoon
0.5g total fat (0.1g saturated fat);
46kJ (11 cal); 0.6g carbohydrate;
0.4g protein; 1g fibre

note Store garlic confit in the
refrigerator. Once opened,
make sure garlic is always
completely covered with oil;
top up with a little more oil
as necessary.
serving ideas To use, squeeze
garlic flesh from the skins and
stir through mayonnaise to
make aïoli, or use in sauces
and dips. Use a little of the
garlic-infused olive oil as a
tasty salad dressing.

onion jam

¼ cup (60ml) olive oil

1kg (2 pounds) brown onions,
sliced thinly

1 sprig fresh rosemary

⅔ cup (160ml) balsamic vinegar

½ cup (110g) firmly packed light
brown sugar

1 Heat oil in large saucepan;
cook onion and rosemary, stirring
occasionally, about 25 minutes or
until onion is soft and browned
lightly. Add vinegar; cook, stirring,
about 5 minutes or until liquid is
absorbed. Add sugar; cook,
stirring, about 10 minutes or
until onion is caramelised and
jam is thick.
2 Spoon hot jam into hot
sterilised jars; seal immediately.
Label and date jars when cold.

prep + cook time 1 hour
makes 2¼ cups
nutritional count per tablespoon
4.6g total fat (0.6g saturated fat);
426kJ (102 cal); 13.4g carbohydrate;
1.2g protein; 1.1g fibre

notes Store onion jam in the
refrigerator. Use a mandoline or
V-slicer to slice onions as thinly
as possible – it's much faster
and easier than using a knife.
serving ideas Serve on burgers
and sandwiches, in quiches and
tarts, or with barbecued meat.

dried fruit relish

2 cups (300g) coarsely chopped dried apricots

2 cups (280g) coarsely chopped dried dates

375g (12 ounces) dried figs, stems removed, chopped finely

3 cups (750ml) boiling water

1½ cups (330g) firmly packed light brown sugar

2¼ cups (310ml) cider vinegar

2 teaspoons coarse cooking salt (kosher salt)

1 Combine fruit and the water in large saucepan; stand 30 minutes.
2 Add remaining ingredients to pan; stir over high heat, without boiling, until sugar dissolves. Bring to the boil. Reduce heat; simmer, uncovered, stirring occasionally, about 40 minutes or until relish is thick.
3 Spoon hot relish into hot sterilised jars; seal immediately. Label and date jars when cold.

prep + cook time 1 hour (+ standing) **makes** 6 cups
nutritional count per tablespoon 0.1g total fat (0g saturated fat); 213kJ (51 cal); 11.7g carbohydrate; 0.5g protein; 1.5g fibre

note Store relish in a cool, dark place for at least one week before opening. Refrigerate after opening.
serving ideas Serve with cheese, pork and ham.

caramelised onion and beetroot relish

2 tablespoons olive oil

4 large brown onions (800g), sliced thinly

1½ cups (330g) firmly packed light brown sugar

1½ cups (375ml) cider vinegar

3 large fresh beetroot (beets) (600g), peeled, grated coarsely

1 teaspoon coarse cooking salt (kosher salt)

½ teaspoon cracked black pepper

1 Heat oil in large saucepan; cook onion, stirring, about 15 minutes or until onion is softened and caramelised.

2 Add remaining ingredients; stir over high heat, without boiling, until sugar dissolves. Bring to the boil. Reduce heat; simmer, uncovered, stirring occasionally, about 30 minutes or until beetroot is tender and relish is thick.

3 Spoon hot relish into hot sterilised jars; seal immediately. Label and date jars when cold.

prep + cook time 1 hour
makes 4 cups
nutritional count per tablespoon
0.8 g total fat (0.1g saturated fat); 184kJ (44 cal); 8.5g carbohydrate; 0.5g protein; 0.6g fibre

notes Wear disposable gloves when peeling beetroot as it will stain your hands.
Store relish in a cool, dark place for at least three weeks before opening. Refrigerate the relish after opening.
serving ideas Serve with steak sandwiches and hamburgers.

indian eggplant relish

3 medium eggplants (900g)

2 teaspoons coarse cooking salt (kosher salt)

2 tablespoons vegetable oil

½ teaspoon yellow mustard seeds

1 large red onion (300g), chopped finely

3 cloves garlic, crushed

2 fresh long green chillies, chopped finely

½ teaspoon cumin seeds

1 large tomato (220g), peeled, chopped finely

⅓ cup loosely packed fresh coriander (cilantro) leaves

¼ cup loosely packed fresh mint leaves

1 teaspoon chilli powder

½ teaspoon ground turmeric

½ teaspoon tamarind concentrate

3 teaspoons coarse cooking salt (kosher salt), extra

1 cup (250ml) water

1 Peel alternate lengthwise strips of skin from eggplants; chop eggplants coarsely. Place eggplant in medium non-metallic bowl; sprinkle with salt, mix well. Stand 10 minutes. Rinse and drain eggplant well; drain on absorbent paper.

2 Heat oil in large frying pan; cook mustard seeds, stirring, until they begin to pop. Add onion, garlic, fresh chilli and cumin seeds; cook, stirring, until onion softens. Add tomato; cook, stirring, about 2 minutes or until tomato softens. Stir in eggplant and remaining ingredients; simmer, covered, over low heat, stirring occasionally, about 25 minutes or until eggplant is tender. Cool 15 minutes, then blend or process eggplant mixture until pulpy.

3 Spoon relish into hot sterilised jars; seal immediately. Label and date jars when cold.

prep + cook time 45 minutes (+ cooling) **makes** 4½ cups
nutritional count per tablespoon 0.7g total fat (0.1g saturated fat); 50kJ (12 cal); 0.9g carbohydrate; 0.3g protein; 0.6g fibre

note The relish can be stored in the refrigerator for up to three weeks.

serving ideas Serve with Indian curries and egg dishes.

corn relish

8 corn cobs (3.2kg), trimmed, kernels removed

2 medium red capsicums (bell peppers) (400g), chopped finely

1 large red onion (300g), chopped finely

2 stalks celery (300g), trimmed, chopped finely

1 cup (220g) white (granulated) sugar

1 tablespoon yellow mustard seeds

3 teaspoons mustard powder

1 teaspoon ground turmeric

2 teaspoons coarse cooking salt (kosher salt)

2 cups (500ml) cider vinegar

1½ tablespoons cornflour (cornstarch)

2 tablespoons water

1 Stir vegetables, sugar, spices, salt and vinegar in large saucepan over high heat, without boiling, until sugar dissolves. Bring to the boil. Reduce heat; simmer, uncovered, stirring occasionally, for 25 minutes.

2 Blend cornflour with the water in small bowl until smooth; stir into vegetable mixture. Cook, stirring, until mixture boils and thickens. Pour into hot sterilised jars; seal immediately. Label and date jars when cold.

prep + cook time 1 hour
makes 8 cups
nutritional count per tablespoon 0.3g total fat (0g saturated fat); 155kJ (37 cal); 6.8g carbohydrate; 1.1g protein; 1.2g fibre

note Relish will keep for several weeks in the refrigerator. Relish can be used straight away.
serving ideas Serve with cold meats or on sandwiches.

sauces

tomato sauce

2 tablespoons olive oil

2 medium brown onions (300g), chopped finely

3 cloves garlic, crushed

4cm (1½-inch) piece fresh ginger (20g), grated

1 teaspoon ground coriander

1kg (2 pounds) ripe egg (plum) tomatoes, chopped coarsely

½ cup (110g) firmly packed light brown sugar

⅓ cup (80ml) red wine vinegar

⅓ cup (80ml) white vinegar

1 teaspoon coarse cooking salt (kosher salt)

1 Heat oil in large saucepan; cook onion, stirring, until softened. Add garlic, ginger and spice; cook, stirring, until fragrant. Stir in remaining ingredients. Bring to the boil. Reduce heat; simmer, uncovered, about 40 minutes or until tomatoes are soft and sauce thickens. Cool 15 minutes.

2 Blend or process mixture, in batches, until smooth; strain sauce through fine sieve into large heatproof bowl, discard solids. Return sauce to pan; bring to the boil, stirring.

3 Pour hot sauce into hot sterilised jars; seal immediately. Label and date jars when cold.

prep + cook time 50 minutes (+ cooling)
makes 3 cups
nutritional count per tablespoon
1.1g total fat (0.1g saturated fat); 117kJ (28 cal); 4g carbohydrate; 0.4g protein; 0.5g fibre

serving ideas Serve with sausages or barbecued meat, or serve as a dipping sauce.
variation For a spicy tomato sauce, add 1 finely chopped fresh long red chilli with the garlic in step 1.

harissa

2 medium red capsicums
(bell peppers) (400g)

2 tablespoons ground cumin

1 tablespoon ground coriander

20 fresh small red thai (serrano)
chillies (110g), stalks removed

10 cloves garlic, quartered

6 fresh coriander (cilantro) roots

1 teaspoon coarse cooking salt
(kosher salt)

2 tablespoons olive oil

1 Preheat oven to 200°C/ 400°F.

2 Quarter capsicums; discard seeds and membranes. Roast capsicum, skin-side up, until skin blisters and blackens. Cover with plastic or paper for 5 minutes, then peel away skin.

3 Meanwhile, dry-fry spices in small frying pan until fragrant.

4 Blend or process capsicum, spices, chillies, garlic, coriander roots and salt until smooth. With motor operating, gradually add oil in a thin, steady stream; blend until combined.

5 Spoon harissa into hot sterilised jars; seal immediately. Label and date jars when cold.

prep + cook time 30 minutes
makes about 1¾ cups
nutritional count per tablespoon
1.8g total fat (0.3g saturated fat);
100kJ (24 cal); 1g carbohydrate;
0.4g protein; 1g fibre

notes Store harissa in the refrigerator. Harissa can be used straight away. The heat of harissa depends on the type and amount of chilli used; increase or decrease the number of chillies used depending on your heat tolerance.
Always wear gloves when handling chillies and it's a good idea to open the windows when blending the chillies to avoid stinging eyes.

serving ideas Serve with or use as a marinade for grilled chicken and meat. Stir a little through yogurt or mayonnaise and serve as a spicy dipping sauce or, if you like it hot, serve it on its own.

smoky tomato sauce

¼ cup (35g) plain (all-purpose) flour

½ cup (40g) loose tea leaves

1kg (2 pounds) ripe egg (plum) tomatoes, halved lengthways

2 tablespoons olive oil

2 medium brown onions (300g), chopped finely

5 cloves garlic, crushed

½ cup (110g) firmly packed light brown sugar

½ cup (125ml) white vinegar

1 teaspoon coarse cooking salt (kosher salt)

1 Line large wok with foil; place flour and tea leaves in base of wok. Heat wok over medium-high heat until smoke appears. Place half the tomatoes, skin-side up, on small oiled wire rack inside wok. Cover wok; cook 10 minutes. Remove from heat; stand, covered, 10 minutes.

2 Heat oil in large saucepan; cook onion and garlic, stirring, until onion softens. Add all of the tomatoes and remaining ingredients; bring to the boil. Reduce heat; simmer, uncovered, stirring occasionally, about 40 minutes or until tomato softens and sauce is thick. Cool 15 minutes.

3 Blend or process tomato mixture, in batches, until smooth. Strain mixture through a fine sieve into large bowl; discard solids. Return to pan; bring to the boil.

4 Pour hot sauce into hot sterilised jars, seal immediately. Label and date jars when cold.

prep + cook time 1¼ hours (+ cooling) **makes** 3 cups
nutritional count per tablespoon 1.1g total fat (0.1g saturated fat); 117kJ (28 cal); 4g carbohydrate; 0.4g protein; 0.5g fibre

notes We used black tea leaves, but you could also use a smoky tea such as lapsang souchong. It's a good idea to do the smoking on the barbecue. Store sauce in the refrigerator.
serving ideas Serve with sausages or barbecued meat, or use a little in dips and sauces.

sweet chilli sauce

200g (6½ ounces) fresh long red chillies, chopped coarsely

1½ cups (330g) caster (superfine) sugar

1½ cups (375ml) white vinegar

4 cloves garlic, peeled

4cm (1½-inch) piece fresh ginger (20g), grated

½ teaspoon coarse cooking salt (kosher salt)

1 Combine ingredients in medium saucepan; stir over high heat, without boiling, until sugar dissolves. Reduce heat; simmer, uncovered, about 45 minutes or until chilli is soft. Cool 10 minutes.
2 Blend or process mixture, in batches, until smooth.
3 Pour sauce into hot sterilised jars; seal immediately. Label and date jars when cold.

prep + cook time 1 hour
makes 1¾ cups
nutritional count per tablespoon 0.1g total fat (0g saturated fat); 33kJ (8 cal); 16.2g carbohydrate; 0.2g protein; 1.1g fibre

notes Wear gloves when preparing the chillies as they can burn your skin. The hotness of the sauce will depend on the type of chillies used.
Store in a cool, dark place for one week before opening. Sauce will keep in a cool, dark place for up to three months; refrigerate after opening. It will keep for several months in the refrigerator.

serving ideas Serve as a dipping sauce with spring rolls, rice paper rolls or dumplings, or use in stir-fries.

barbecue sauce

2 tablespoons olive oil

2 medium brown onions (300g), chopped finely

5 cloves garlic, crushed

1kg (2 pounds) ripe egg (plum) tomatoes, chopped coarsely

¾ cup (165g) firmly packed light brown sugar

½ cup (125ml) malt vinegar

⅓ cup (80ml) worcestershire sauce

1 teaspoon coarse cooking salt (kosher salt)

1 Heat oil in large saucepan; cook onion, stirring, until softened. Add garlic; cook, stirring, until fragrant. Stir in remaining ingredients. Bring to the boil. Reduce heat; simmer, uncovered, about 1 hour or until tomatoes are soft and sauce is thickened. Cool 15 minutes.

2 Blend or process mixture, in batches, until smooth. Strain sauce through fine sieve into large heatproof bowl. Return sauce to pan; bring to the boil, stirring.

3 Pour hot sauce into hot sterilised jars; seal immediately. Label and date jars when cold.

prep + cook time 1½ hours (+ cooling) **makes** 2¼ cups **nutritional count per tablespoon** 1.4g total fat (0.2g saturated fat); 201kJ (48 cal); 7.9g carbohydrate; 0.6g protein; 0.7g fibre

note It's much easier to check the consistency of the sauce after it has been blended and strained. If the sauce is too thin, return the sauce to the pan, bring it to the boil, then reduce the heat and simmer, uncovered, until reduced to about 2¼ cups.
serving ideas Serve with barbecued meats or use it in meat marinades and as a base on pizzas.

traditional italian tomato pasta sauce

10kg (20 pounds) ripe egg (plum) tomatoes

1 cup firmly packed fresh basil leaves

1 Trim tops from tomatoes; cut tomatoes in half lengthways. Scrape out seeds.
2 Divide tomato halves into two large saucepans, or place in a large boiler; cook, covered, over low heat, stirring occasionally, about 30 minutes or until tomatoes begin to soften. Cool 10 minutes. Using a jug, carefully skim excess water from the surface of the tomatoes (about 1½ cups from each pan). Discard water.

3 Blend or process tomatoes, in batches, until smooth. Push tomato puree through a fine sieve, in batches, into large bowl or jug; discard solids.
4 Pour tomato puree into hot sterilised bottles or jars (do not completely fill bottles or jars to the top – leave at least 2cm of space); push three basil leaves into each bottle. Seal immediately.
5 Wrap bottles in tea towels or several layers of newspaper; pack upright bottles tightly into large tall saucepan or boiler. Cover bottles with boiling water; bring to the boil. Boil for 1 hour, covered, replenishing water, as necessary, to maintain level. Cool bottles in water. Label and date bottles.

prep + cook time 3 hours (+ cooling) **makes** 22 cups **nutritional count per ½ cup** 0.1g total fat (0g saturated fat); 63kJ (15 cal); 1.7g carbohydrate; 0.9g protein; 1.1g fibre

notes Store in a cool, dark place for up to 12 months; refrigerate after opening.

If you have one, push the cooked tomato mixture through a mouli or food mill to remove the tomato skins, instead of following instructions for step 3; there is no need to blend the mixture first if pushing it through a mouli. Continue recipe from step 4.

We used very ripe egg tomatoes. Specially grown 'sauce' tomatoes are available from local markets in the late summer months.

It is best to use either 2-cup (500ml) jars (serves 4) or 3-cup (750ml) jars (serves 6).

serving ideas Serve over cooked pasta or use as a base for soups, bolognese sauce and lasagne.

For a classic Sicilian pasta, fry a finely chopped small onion in a medium saucepan; add the sauce. Simmer, uncovered, about 15 minutes or until sauce is thick and a rich red colour. Stir in a handful of frozen peas and season to taste. Toss sauce through cooked penne pasta.

drinks

pomegranate and rhubarb cordial

600g (1¼ pounds) trimmed rhubarb, chopped coarsely

⅓ cup (80ml) water

2½ cups (625ml) pomegranate pulp

1 cup (220g) caster (superfine) sugar

1 teaspoon citric acid

prep + cook time 35 minutes (+ standing)
makes 2½ cups
nutritional count per tablespoon (undiluted)
0.1g total fat (0g saturated fat); 46kJ
(11 cal); 8.8g carbohydrate; 0.4g protein;
1g fibre

1 Combine rhubarb and the water in medium saucepan; bring to the boil. Reduce heat; simmer, covered, about 10 minutes or until mixture is pulpy. Pour mixture through muslin-lined sieve into medium bowl. Stand 20 minutes, then squeeze muslin to extract more juice.
2 Meanwhile, place pomegranate in muslin-lined sieve over small bowl; squeeze muslin to extract as much juice as possible (you will need 1 cup juice). Discard seeds (or save for another use).
3 Combine fruit juices, sugar and citric acid in medium saucepan; stir over high heat, without boiling, until sugar dissolves. Bring to the boil.
4 Pour hot syrup into hot sterilised bottles; seal immediately. Label and date bottles when cold.

notes You will need about 1 bunch of rhubarb (use only the reddest stems) and 3 large pomegranates for this recipe. Store in the refrigerator for up to two weeks or freeze cordial in plastic bottles for up to three months; make sure you leave at least 2cm (¾ inch) of space in the bottles to allow for expansion of liquid as it freezes.

serving ideas Dilute the cordial with an equal amount of iced water or chilled sparkling mineral water. Serve in glasses with ice-blocks and mint leaves; or use in cocktails.
It's also delicious served undiluted, as a sauce, over ice-cream. Use the leftover pomegranate seeds in salads or sprinkle over desserts.

cherries in brandy

1kg (2 pounds) fresh cherries, stalks on

1 cinnamon stick

1½ cups (330g) caster (superfine) sugar

2 cups (500ml) brandy, approximately

1 Wash and dry cherries well. Place cherries and cinnamon in 1.5 litre (6-cup) sterilised jar; add sugar and enough brandy to cover cherries.
2 Seal jar; invert jar several times to help dissolve the sugar. Label and date jar.

prep time 10 minutes (+ standing)
makes 6 cups
nutritional count per ¼ cup
0.1g total fat (0g saturated fat); 468kJ (112 cal); 17.3g carbohydrate; 0.3g protein; 0.5g fibre

notes Store cherries in a cool, dark place for at least 2 months before opening. Invert the jar every few days to help dissolve the sugar. Refrigerate after opening.
Choose unblemished cherries. Remove the stalks from the cherries if you like. Pack cherries tightly into jar but be gentle to avoid bruising. Cherries will float to the surface; to keep them submerged, place a sealed small plastic bag filled with water on top of the cherries before closing the jar.

serving idea Serve spoonfuls of cherries in small glasses with vanilla ice-cream; it also goes well with coffee. Drink the flavoured brandy as you would a liqueur.

limoncello

8 medium lemons (1.1kg)

3 cups (750ml) vodka

1 cup (220g) caster (superfine) sugar

2 cups (500ml) water

1 Using a vegetable peeler, peel lemons thinly; discard any white pith from rind. Combine rind and vodka in 1-litre (4-cup) sterilised jar; seal. Stand jar in a cool, dark place for six days, shaking jar once a day.

2 To make sugar syrup, combine sugar and the water in medium saucepan; stir over high heat, without boiling, until sugar dissolves. Bring to the boil; remove from heat, cool.

3 Strain vodka through fine sieve into large bowl or jug; discard rind. Stir sugar syrup into vodka.

4 Pour limoncello into sterilised bottles; seal immediately. Label and date bottle. Refrigerate until cold before serving.

prep + cook time 30 minutes (+ standing & cooling)
makes 5 cups
nutritional count per tablespoon 0g total fat (0g saturated fat); 180kJ (43 cal); 4g carbohydrate; 0.1g protein; 0.4g fibre

note Store limoncello in the refrigerator. We use the peel only from the lemons for this recipe. Once peeled, the lemons need to be refrigerated and used quickly; try making lemon curd (page 10) or freeze the juice in an ice-cube tray.

serving ideas Serve in chilled shot glasses or over ice, or serve over ice-cream, gelato or sorbet for a delicious dessert.

glossary

ALLSPICE also called pimento or jamaican pepper, tastes like a combination of nutmeg, cumin, clove and cinnamon – all spices. Available in ground form, or as berries, from good spice shops.

BAY LEAF aromatic leaves from the bay tree. Available fresh and dried.

BUTTER use salted or unsalted (sweet) butter; 125g is equal to one stick (4 ounces) of butter.

unsalted butter simply has no added salt. It is mainly used when making citrus or passionfruit curd.

CARDAMOM available in pod, seed or ground form. It has a distinctive aromatic, sweetly rich flavour and is one of the world's most expensive spices.

CAYENNE PEPPER see chilli.

CHERRIES, GLACÉ cooked in a heavy sugar syrup then dried.

CHILLI available in many different types and sizes. Use rubber gloves when seeding and chopping fresh chillies as they can burn your skin. Generally, the smaller the chilli, the hotter it is.

cayenne pepper a long, thin-fleshed, extremely hot red chilli usually sold dried and ground.

dried flakes deep-red, dehydrated chilli slices and whole seeds.

kashmiri these do not necessarily come from Kashmir; they are a popular Indian chilli with a high colour content, making the food they are used in a bright red colour without adding too much heat.

long green any unripened chilli; also some particular varieties that are ripe when green, such as jalapeño, habanero, poblano or serrano.

long red available both fresh and dried; a generic term used for any moderately hot, long (about 6cm to 8cm), thin, chilli.

powder the Asian variety, made from dried ground red thai chillies, is the hottest; substitute for fresh chillies in the proportion of ½ teaspoon ground chilli powder to 1 medium chopped fresh chilli.

red thai also known as 'scuds'; small, very hot and bright red in colour.

CINNAMON dried inner bark of the shoots of the cinnamon tree; available in stick (quill) or ground form.

CITRIC ACID is commonly found in most fruits, especially limes and lemons. Commercial citric acid accentuates the acid flavour of fruit, however, it is not a preservative.

CLOVES dried flower buds of a tropical tree; can be used whole or in ground form. Has a distinctively pungent and 'spicy' scent and flavour.

COCONUT, FLAKED dried, flaked, coconut flesh.

CORIANDER also known as pak chee, cilantro or chinese parsley; bright-green leafy herb with a pungent flavour. Both the stems and roots of coriander are used in cooking; wash well before using. Wash the coriander under cold water, removing any dirt clinging to the roots; scrape the roots with a small flat knife to remove some of the outer fibrous skin. Chop coriander roots and stems together to obtain the amount specified in the recipe. Also available ground or as seeds; these should not be substituted for fresh coriander as the tastes are completely different.

CORNFLOUR (cornstarch) used as a thickening agent. Available as 100% maize (corn) and wheaten cornflour.

CUCUMBER, BABY the young fruit of a small variety of dark green cucumber grown especially for pickling.

cucumber, lebanese short, slender and thin-skinned. Probably the most popular variety because of its tender, edible skin, tiny seeds and sweet, fresh taste.

CUMIN also known as zeera or comino; this tiny dried seed has a spicy, nutty flavour. Available in seed form or dried and ground.

CURRY POWDER a blend of ground spices consisting of dried coriander, chilli, cinnamon, cumin, fenugreek, fennel, mace, cardamom and turmeric. Available in mild and hot varieties.

DILL this herb develops fine feathery leaves from a single stalk. Sweet and slightly tangy in flavour, dill has the best flavour when used fresh but dried dill is also available.

FENUGREEK the leaves and seeds are available dried or ground; the seeds have a bitter taste. Often used in curries.

FIVE-SPICE POWDER (chinese five-spice) a fragrant mixture of ground cinnamon, cloves, star anise, sichuan pepper and fennel seeds.

FLAT-LEAF PARSLEY also known as continental or italian parsley.

FLOUR, PLAIN an all-purpose flour made from wheat.

GARAM MASALA a blend of spices based on varying proportions of cloves, cardamom, cinnamon, fennel, cumin and coriander, roasted and ground together. Black pepper and chilli can be added for a hotter version.

GHERKIN a very small variety of pickled cucumber; when pickled with dill it is known as a dill pickle.

GINGER

glacé fresh ginger root preserved in sugar syrup. Crystallised ginger can be substituted if rinsed with warm water and dried before using.

ground also powdered ginger; cannot be substituted for fresh ginger.

GREEN MANGO sour and crunchy, green mangoes are just immature fruit. They will keep, wrapped in plastic, in the fridge for up to two weeks.

HERBS, DRIED MIXED a blend of dried crushed thyme, rosemary, marjoram, basil, oregano and sage.

JAMSETTA a powdered pectin product that helps set jam.

MANDARIN a small, loose-skinned citrus fruit also known as tangerine.

MINT a herb that includes many varieties including spearmint, common mint and peppermint. Spearmint has long, smooth leaves, and is the one greengrocers sell, while common mint, with rounded, pebbly leaves, is the one that most people grow. Spearmint has the stronger flavour.

MIXED SPICE a blend of ground spices usually consisting of cinnamon, allspice and nutmeg.

MUSHROOMS, BUTTON small, cultivated white mushrooms with a delicate, subtle flavour.

MUSTARD

powder finely ground yellow (white) mustard seeds.

seeds yellow mustard seeds, also known as white mustard seeds, are ground and used for mustard powder and in most prepared mustards. Black are also known as brown mustard seeds; they are more pungent than the yellow variety and are used in curries. Available from major supermarkets and health-food shops.

NECTARINES a variety of peach; available with white or yellow flesh. They can be either clingstone (when cut, the flesh clings to the stone) or freestone (when cut, the flesh will fall or twist cleanly away from the stone).

NUTMEG the dried nut of an evergreen tree native to Indonesia; it is available in ground form or you can grate your own with a fine grater.

OIL

olive made from the first pressing of ripened olives. Extra virgin and virgin are the best, while extra light or light refers to taste, not fat levels.

vegetable any of a number of oils that have been sourced from plants rather than animal fats.

OLIVES

black have a richer and more mellow flavour than the green ones and are softer in texture. Sold either plain or in a piquant marinade.

green those harvested before fully ripened and are, as a rule, denser and more bitter than their black relatives.

kalamata small, sharp-tasting, brine-cured black olives.

niçoise small black olives.

pimento-stuffed a green olive with a lively, briny bitterness containing a morsel of capsicum (pepper), which adds a flash of colour.

ORANGE BLOSSOM WATER also known as orange flower water; a concentrated flavouring made from orange blossoms. Available from Middle-Eastern food stores and some supermarkets and delicatessens. It can not be substituted with citrus flavouring, as the tastes are completely different.

OREGANO a herb, also known as wild marjoram; has a woody stalk with clumps of tiny, dark green leaves that have a pungent, peppery flavour and are used fresh or dried.

PAPRIKA ground dried sweet red capsicum (pepper); there are many types available, including sweet, hot, mild and smoked.

PATTY-PAN SQUASH also known as crookneck or custard marrow pumpkin; a round, slightly flat, summer squash being yellow to pale-green in colour and having a scalloped edge. Harvested young, it has a firm white flesh and a distinct flavour.

PEACHES come in yellow and white varieties, both of which can be either clingstone or freestone, defined by whether the flesh separates cleanly from the stone. See also nectarines.

PEPPERCORN MEDLEY this is a combination of black, white and green peppercorns; it is fine to just use the same amount of black peppercorns if you can't get the medley. Available from most major supermarkets.

PLOUGHMAN'S LUNCH a hearty, cold lunch for the labourer. It consists of thick slices of crusty bread, cheese plus pickled onions and chutney or pickles, but this can vary considerably. It may also contain a selection of cold meats.

PLUMS can be clingstone or freestone, defined by whether the flesh separates cleanly from the stone. See also nectarines.

PUMPKIN a large rounded or elongated thick-skinned fruit, which is usually orange or yellow, though may also be dark green; has an edible flesh beneath its thick skin, which contains many seeds. May also be known as gourd, squash or winter squash.

RAISINS dried sweet grapes.

RED CABBAGE is good raw in salads; otherwise, cook slowly and gently with a minimum of water plus an acid ingredient such as apple, vinegar or wine. The acid component is needed because plain water may be alkaline, which turns red cabbage a discouraging blue-green colour with a flavour to match.

ROSEMARY a woody, evergreen Mediterranean herb with strong, resinous fragrance and flavour.

ROSEWATER called gulab in India, this is distilled from rose petals, and used in the Middle East, North Africa, and India to flavour desserts. Don't confuse this with rose essence, which is more concentrated.

SALT

coarse cooking is coarser than table salt, but not as large-flaked as sea salt: it is sold in most supermarkets.

rock sold in large crystals, rock salt has a greyish hue because it is unrefined.

SAUCES

chilli bean a hot, spicy, salty sauce made from fermented broad beans, soya beans, rice, chillies and spices.

fish also called nam pla or nuoc nam; is made from pulverised salted fermented fish, most often anchovies. Has a pungent smell and strong taste; use sparingly.

soy also known as sieu, is made from fermented soya beans. Several variations are available in most supermarkets and Asian food stores.
dark soy is deep brown, almost black in colour; rich, with a thicker consistency than other types. Pungent but not particularly salty.
japanese soy an all-purpose low-sodium sauce made with more wheat content than its Chinese counterparts; fermented in barrels and aged.
light soy fairly thin in consistency and, while paler than the others, the saltiest tasting; used in dishes in which the natural colour of the ingredients is to be maintained. Don't confuse with salt-reduced or low-sodium soy sauces.

sweet chilli a mild, Thai sauce made with chillies, sugar, garlic and vinegar.

Tabasco brand name of an extremely fiery sauce made from vinegar, thai red chillies and salt.

worcestershire made from soy sauce, garlic, tamarind, onions, molasses, lime, anchovies, vinegar and other seasonings.

SICHUAN PEPPERCORNS also known as szechuan or chinese pepper, native to the Sichuan province of China. Not related to the peppercorn family, but the small, red-brown sichuan berries look like black peppercorns and have a distinctive peppery-lemon flavour and aroma. Should be dry-roasted to bring out their full flavour.

SUGAR
brown *light brown* is an extremely soft, finely granulated sugar retaining molasses for its characteristic colour and flavour. *Dark brown* is moist with a rich, distinctive full flavour coming from natural molasses syrup.

caster also known as superfine or finely granulated table sugar.

palm sugar also known as nam tan pip, jaggery, jawa or gula melaka; made from the sap of the sugar palm tree. Light brown to black in colour and usually sold in rock-hard cakes. Substitute with brown sugar.

raw a natural brown granulated sugar.

white a coarse, granulated table sugar, also known as crystal sugar.

SULTANAS dried grapes, also known as golden raisins.

SUMAC a purple-red, astringent spice ground from berries growing on shrubs that flourish wild around the Mediterranean; adds a tart, lemony flavour. Available from Middle-Eastern food stores and major supermarkets.

SWEDE also known as rutabaga or neeps; has a purple-hued, creamy-coloured skin and creamy-coloured flesh. Is stronger and sweeter in flavour than the turnip, with a fresh nutty taste and a slightly crisp texture, even when cooked. Its creamy white flesh turns golden when cooked.

TAMARILLO also known as tree tomato. A smooth-skinned purple, red, orange or yellow fruit, (the yellow variety tending to be a bit sweeter). The flesh is black or orange (the darker the peel, the darker the flesh) surrounding a nest of seeds. It's more acidic than sweet, and tastes a bit like a tomato. It's best if it's peeled and cooked before eating.

TAMARIND the tamarind tree produces clusters of hairy brown pods, each of which is filled with seeds and a viscous pulp that are dried and pressed into the blocks of tamarind found in Asian food shops. Gives a sour, tart taste to dishes.

tamarind concentrate commercial distillation of tamarind pulp into a condensed paste. Used straight from the container, with no soaking or straining required; can be diluted with water according to taste. Found in Asian food stores and supermarkets.

TANGELO a loose-skinned, juicy, sweetly-tart citrus fruit with few seeds.

TARRAGON an aromatic herb with dark green leaves and an anise-like flavour. Store stems down in a glass of water with a plastic bag on top. Known as the 'king of herbs' in France.

TARTARIC ACID a natural food acid found in many plants especially grapes. It has a taste that is naturally sour and gives foods a sharp, tart flavour. Helps to set and preserve foods. It is also an ingredient in cream of tartar, and is found in some brands of baking powder.

THYME a member of the mint family, it has tiny grey-green leaves that give off a pungent minty, light-lemon aroma. Fresh thyme should be stored in the refrigerator, wrapped in a damp paper towel and placed in a sealed bag for no more than a few days.

lemon thyme a herb with a lemony scent, which is due to the high level of citral in its leaves – an oil also found in lemon, orange, verbena and lemon grass. The citrus scent is enhanced by crushing the leaves in your hands before using the herb.

TOMATOES, SEMI-DRIED partially dried tomato pieces in olive oil; softer and juicier than sun-dried, these are not a preserve thus do not keep as long as sun-dried.

TREACLE a concentrated, refined sugar syrup with a distinctive flavour and dark black colour; similar to molasses but is less bitter and viscous.

TURMERIC, GROUND a member of the ginger family, its root is dried and ground, resulting in the rich yellow powder that adds a characteristic golden colour to foods. It is intensely pungent in taste, but not hot.

VINEGAR
balsamic originally from Modena, Italy, there are now many balsamic vinegars on the market ranging in pungency and quality depending on how long they have been aged. Made from a regional wine of white Trebbiano grapes specially processed and aged in antique wooden casks to give the exquisite pungent flavour. It is a deep rich brown colour with a sweet and sour flavour. Quality can be determined up to a point by price; use the most expensive sparingly.

malt (brown malt) is made from fermented malt and beech shavings.

cider (apple cider) made from fermented apples.

red wine based on fermented red wine.

rice wine made from rice wine lees (sediment left after fermentation), salt and alcohol.

sherry made from a blend of wines and left in wood vats to mature where they develop a rich mellow flavour.

white made from spirit of cane sugar.

white wine made from a blend of white wines.

ZUCCHINI also known as courgette; small, pale- or dark-green, yellow or white vegetable belonging to the squash family. Harvested when young, its edible flowers can be stuffed then deep-fried or oven-baked to make a delicious appetiser. The stem of the zucchini is the baby zucchini attached to the flower.

conversion chart

MEASURES

One Australian metric measuring cup holds approximately 250ml; one Australian metric tablespoon holds 20ml; one Australian metric teaspoon holds 5ml.

The difference between one country's measuring cups and another's is within a two- or three-teaspoon variance, and will not affect your cooking results. North America, New Zealand and the United Kingdom use a 15ml tablespoon.

All cup and spoon measurements are level. The most accurate way of measuring dry ingredients is to weigh them. When measuring liquids, use a clear glass or plastic jug with the metric markings.

We use large eggs with an average weight of 60g.

DRY MEASURES

METRIC	IMPERIAL
15g	½oz
30g	1oz
60g	2oz
90g	3oz
125g	4oz (¼lb)
155g	5oz
185g	6oz
220g	7oz
250g	8oz (½lb)
280g	9oz
315g	10oz
345g	11oz
375g	12oz (¾lb)
410g	13oz
440g	14oz
470g	15oz
500g	16oz (1lb)
750g	24oz (1½lb)
1kg	32oz (2lb)

LIQUID MEASURES

METRIC	IMPERIAL
30ml	1 fluid oz
60ml	2 fluid oz
100ml	3 fluid oz
125ml	4 fluid oz
150ml	5 fluid oz
190ml	6 fluid oz
250ml	8 fluid oz
300ml	10 fluid oz
500ml	16 fluid oz
600ml	20 fluid oz
1000ml (1 litre)	1¾ pints

LENGTH MEASURES

METRIC	IMPERIAL
3mm	⅛in
6mm	¼in
1cm	½in
2cm	¾in
2.5cm	1in
5cm	2in
6cm	2½in
8cm	3in
10cm	4in
13cm	5in
15cm	6in
18cm	7in
20cm	8in
23cm	9in
25cm	10in
28cm	11in
30cm	12in (1ft)

OVEN TEMPERATURES

The oven temperatures in this book are for conventional ovens; if you have a fan-forced oven, decrease the temperature by 10-20 degrees.

	°C (CELSIUS)	°F (FAHRENHEIT)
Very slow	120	250
Slow	150	300
Moderately slow	160	325
Moderate	180	350
Moderately hot	200	400
Hot	220	425
Very hot	240	475

The imperial measurements used in these recipes are approximate only. Measurements for cake pans are approximate only. Using same-shaped cake pans of a similar size should not affect the outcome of your baking. We measure the inside top of the cake pan to determine sizes.

index

A

any berry jam 29
apple
    and blueberry jam 17
    and passionfruit jelly 45
    jelly 45
apricot
    and vanilla bean jam 13
    dried, and mandarin jam 25

B

banana jam 29
barbecue sauce 104
beetroot and caramelised onion relish 91
beetroot chutney 48
berry jam, any 29
blueberry and apple jam 17
brandy, cherries in 111
bread and butter pickle 75

C

caramelised onion and beetroot relish 91
carrot and orange marmalade 41
Champagne, peach and raspberry jam 22
cherries in brandy 111
cherry jam 18
chilli jam 63
chilli sauce, sweet 103
chillies, pickled 76
chow chow 72
chunky fig and vanilla jam 26
chutney
    beetroot 48
    green mango 52
    green tomato 51
    indian tamarind 64
    mango 56
    peach and ginger 60
    sweet fruit 59
    watermelon rind 55
classic fruit mince 25
confit, garlic 87
conserve, strawberry and orange 13
cordial, pomegranate and rhubarb 108
    coriander, orange and ginger marmalade 38

corn relish 95
cracked olives 83
cranberry and lemon marmalade 34
cumquat marmalade 38
curd, lemon 10

D

dried fruit relish 88

E

eggplant relish, indian 92

F

fig and vanilla jam, chunky 26
fruit
    chutney, sweet 59
    mince, classic 25
    relish, dried 88

G

garlic confit 87
ginger
    and peach chutney 60
    and rhubarb jam 14
    orange and coriander marmalade 38
grape jelly 46
green mango chutney 52
green tomato chutney 51
green tomato jam 26

H

harissa 99

I

indian eggplant relish 92
indian tamarind chutney 64

J

jam
    any berry 29
    apricot and vanilla bean 13
    banana 29
    blueberry and apple 17
    cherry 18
    chilli 63
    chunky fig and vanilla 26

fig and vanilla, chunky 26
green tomato 26
mandarin and dried apricot 25
mango and strawberry 22
onion 87
peach, raspberry and Champagne 22
raspberry and mint 18
rhubarb and ginger 14
spiced plum and port 17
strawberry and orange conserve 13
jelly
    apple 45
    apple and passionfruit 45
    grape 46
    mint 42

L

lemon
    and cranberry marmalade 34
    curd 10
    limoncello 112
    preserved 80
limoncello 112

M

mandarin
    and dried apricot jam 25
    marmalade 34
mango
    and strawberry jam 22
    chutney 56
    chutney, green 52
marmalade
    cranberry and lemon 34
    cumquat 38
    mandarin 34
    master orange 37
    orange and carrot 41
    orange, coriander and ginger 38
    overnight three-citrus processor 30
    rhubarb and orange 33
    seville orange 33
    thick-cut dark whisky 41
master orange marmalade 37
mint
    and raspberry jam 18
    jelly 42
mustard pickles, sweet 79

O

olives, cracked 83

onion
    and beetroot relish, caramelised 91
    jam 87
    pickled 84
orange
    and carrot marmalade 41
    and rhubarb marmalade 33
    coriander and ginger marmalade 38
    conserve, strawberry and 13
    marmalade, master 37
    marmalade, seville 33
    whisky marmalade, thick-cut dark 41
oven-dried tomatoes 67
overnight three-citrus processor
    marmalade 30

P

passionfruit and apple jelly 45
pasta sauce, traditional italian tomato
    107
pasta, classic sicilian (serving idea) 107
paste, quince 21
peach and ginger chutney 60
peach, raspberry and Champagne
    jam 22
piccalilli 71
pickles
    bread and butter 75
    chow chow 72
    piccalilli 71
    ploughman's 68
    sweet mustard 79
pickled chillies 76
pickled onions 84
ploughman's pickle 68
plum and port jam, spiced 17
pomegranate and rhubarb cordial 108
preserved lemons 80
processor marmalade, overnight
    three-citrus 30

Q

quince paste 21

R

raspberry
    and mint jam 18
    peach and Champagne jam 22
relish
    caramelised onion and beetroot 91
    corn 95

dried fruit 88
indian eggplant 92
rhubarb
    and ginger jam 14
    and orange marmalade 33
    and pomegranate cordial 108

S

sauce
    barbecue 104
    smoky tomato 100
    spicy tomato (variation) 96
    sweet chilli 103
    tomato 96
    traditional italian tomato pasta 107
seville orange marmalade 33
smoky tomato sauce 100
spiced plum and port jam 17
spicy tomato sauce (variation) 96
strawberry
    and mango jam 22
    and orange conserve 13
sweet chilli sauce 103
sweet fruit chutney 59
sweet mustard pickles 79

T

tamarind chutney, indian 64
thick-cut dark whisky marmalade 41
tomato
    chutney, green 51
    jam, green 26
    pasta sauce, traditional italian 107
    sauce 96
    sauce, smoky 100
    sauce, spicy (variation) 96
tomatoes, oven-dried 67
traditional italian tomato pasta sauce
    107

V

vanilla and chunky fig jam 26
vanilla bean and apricot jam 13

W

watermelon rind chutney 55
whisky marmalade, thick-cut dark 41

First published in 2011 by ACP Magazines Ltd,

a division of Nine Entertainment Co.

54 Park St, Sydney

GPO Box 4088, Sydney, NSW 2001.

phone (02) 9282 8618; fax (02) 9267 9438

acpbooks@acpmagazines.com.au; www.acpbooks.com.au

ACP BOOKS

General Manager - Christine Whiston

Editor-in-Chief - Susan Tomnay

Creative Director - Hieu Chi Nguyen

Food Director - Pamela Clark

Published and Distributed in the United Kingdom by Octopus Publishing Group

Endeavour House

189 Shaftesbury Avenue

London WC2H 8JY

United Kingdom

phone (+44)(0)207 632 5400; fax (+44)(0)207 632 5405

info@octopus-publishing.co.uk;

www.octopusbooks.co.uk

Printed by Toppan Printing Co., China

International foreign language rights, Brian Cearnes, ACP Books bcearnes@acpmagazines.com.au

A catalogue record for this book is available from the British Library.
ISBN 978-1-907428-46-3 (pbk.)

© ACP Magazines Ltd 2011

ABN 18 053 273 546